# In Spirit, and in Truth.

CHARISMATIC WORSHIP
AND THE
REFORMED TRADITION

# In

# Spirit, and in

# Truth.

## CHARISMATIC WORSHIP
## AND THE
## REFORMED TRADITION

by
### CALVIN H. CHAMBERS

DORRANCE & COMPANY • Ardmore, Pennsylvania

Selections from *The Gifts of the Spirit and the Body of Christ*, edited by Elmo Agrimson, copyright 1974, reprinted by permission of Augsburg Publishing House.

Selections from *Worship in Word and Sacrament* by Ernest B. Kroenker © 1959 Concordia Publishing House. Used by permission.

Scriptural passages are paraphrased translations made by Calvin Chambers.

To my wife Alice

whose constant love and encouragement have enabled
me to undertake this book

and to

the many brothers and sisters in Christ who have
helped me discover the truths
expressed in these pages

# Contents

# Foreword

The charismatic renewal, which has affected all the historic churches since 1960, is not merely a movement to initiate a Spirit-filled consciousness in the Church. It is fundamentally a renewal of worship, which is one of the highest acts of service a Christian can offer to God. It is a witness to the reality of apostolic joy in the Lord, which becomes meaningful only when the Holy Spirit is permitted to activate the gifts of Christ in his people. Worship is an outward action in which the Christian engages in joyful praise to the Redeemer who is present in our midst. The preached Word, the Word sung and read, the sacrament of the Lord's Supper—the Word symbolized—must center around the risen Christ and all we have in and through him. As the Spirit releases himself in the worship of a living congregation, the gifts of wisdom, knowledge, discerning of spirits, faith, healing, miracles, tongues, interpretation, and prophecy become part of the service. Instead of the minister being the pivotal point around which the worship service moves, the laity—the priests of God—join together with the pastor in offering that kind of praise which truly glorifies him.

There are some who feel that the restoration of Pentecostal gifts and forms of worship are contrary to the spirit of the Reformation. This is not true. The Reformed church, which is centered in the Word of God, will find that the gifts of the Spirit, if utilized properly, can enrich the worship service, making it a dynamic experience of Christ present with his people.

The purpose of this book is to show that worship in Spirit and in truth hold together the spontaneous element in harmony with the unchangeable truths of the Christian faith. The

Reformation was an attempt to model worship after the practices of the early Church. It unfortunately missed out on some of the dynamic aspects of early church worship, about which we read in the New Testament. The charismatic renewal is not an attempt to sweep aside the historic witness of the Reformation. It is, rather, a witness to the need for the twentieth-century Church to hold spirit and truth together. In so doing, our services will be revitalized so that they become an aspect of Christian living that is anticipated week by week by all the people of God.

This book tells the story of one congregation that discovered in a progressive way the joy of worshiping God, governed by the apostolic witness of the New Testament in conjunction with the development of worship as it has taken place down through the centuries. God is the living Spirit, who is constantly on the move, leading his people into fresh discoveries of his love and power. It is my prayer that those who read this volume will realize that God, who has revealed himself in the past, is seeking today to revive our worship life with reality. This will take place as the Spirit is permitted to revitalize old forms and to introduce new ones.

# Preface

THE REFORMATION WAS perhaps the most radical spiritual movement in the history of the Church, apart from the apostolic community which lived in the full light of the resurrection of Jesus Christ. This "radicalism" was not, however, an attempt to reshape the Church according to the dictates of sixteenth-century life. Rather, it was a movement back to the Scriptures to a rediscovery of an understanding of the Christian faith, which was centered solely in the worship of God as revealed in Jesus. The Reformers stripped away from medieval worship everything that they felt minimized the Gospel, and the grace of God which flows through that Gospel. It is difficult for us in the twentieth century to imagine the radical nature of Calvin's approach. The laity were given back their rightful place in the church and in the worship of God, participating in singing, offering of prayer, hearing the Word of God, and observing the sacraments. The services were so alive with meaning that it was nothing for Reformed Christians to join together in worship that lasted two hours or more. It was a time of joyous rediscovery of the greatness of God, an opening of the heart in praise, stimulated by the exciting good news of full salvation in Jesus Christ.

It would be a wonderful thing if the Reformed church throughout the past four centuries had continued to find worship as exciting and relevant as the Reformers and their contemporaries. While it is true that some attempts have been made to reform worship in the Church, it has been inadequate, especially in the light of the current needs of twentieth-century man. Instead of reexamining the Scriptures, many modern liturgists have simply redefined the nature of worship in terms of historic practices that were initiated at the time of the Reformation. Surely this is not what is meant by being a reformed Christian. The principle of Reformation theology, which needs to be constantly recovered, is centered in the need for continual re-formation of church life. Reformed and reforming is glibly espoused by many churchmen today, but very little is done to implement it. Most of our twentieth-century worship services either perpetuate archaic forms, or they attempt a contemporary remodeling of worship, which is based largely upon nonbiblical norms.

There is a vital need for the Church today to reexamine the early Christian community and to enter into the dynamic mode of expression that characterized the Christians of the first century, who were overpowered by the marvelous reality of the presence of God in their midst. The words of Charles Erdman need to be taken seriously as we attempt to make our worship services what they are meant to be for those who know the reality of Jesus Christ:

> There may be too much religious fervour and excitement in some religious gatherings but surely not in many, and most churches need to pray earnestly for a new moving and inspiration of the Holy Spirit in order that the hearts of the worshippers may know something of the passion, the joy, the rapture, the exultation, the triumphant hope, which was the common experience of the early Church, even in Corinth.[1]

---

1. Charles Erdman, *1 Corinthians* (Philadelphia: The Westminster Press, 1938), p. 131.

# Introduction:
# Developing a Charismatic Congregation Worshiping in the Reformed Tradition

THE WESTMINSTER Fellowship of New Westminster, B.C., Canada, came into existence as the result of a controversy that centered around the question of religious freedom. A considerable segment of the congregation, which had been part of First Presbyterian Church, wanted to remain Presbyterian in allegiance; and yet they had entered into a fresh new discovery of the power of the Holy Spirit. This discovery of the reality of Jesus through spiritual renewal in the Holy Spirit expressed itself not only in a manifestation of the gifts of the Spirit as listed in 1 Corinthians 12, but in a deeper grasp of what it means to worship "in spirit and in truth."

In this new congregation, which emerged in 1971, an experiment in renewal took place that centered essentially on the reformation of worship, joined with an understanding of what it means to witness in evangelism and social action. The chief concern was to be governed by the Word of God, so that the congregation did not consider itself a contemporary religious movement experimenting with change and diversity for their own sakes. Through prayer and study on the part of leaders and laity, the Spirit led them into an understanding of what the Church was meant to be in the light of Scripture and the contemporary situation in which the Church found itself.

Five aspects of New Testament church life impressed themselves upon the leadership of the congregation. There was a reaffirmation that the Church must be biblical and reformed, catholic and charismatic, and involved in mission. A concerted effort was made to understand the meaning of these terms, relating them in a positive way to the developing life of the new Fellowship.

First, there was the awareness that the Bible provides the guidelines by which Christians may understand the nature of worship. Nowhere in the New Testament is a pattern for worship laid down as authoritative for all time, but the overall spirit is that of Jesus' teaching when he made it clear to the woman at the well of Sychar: "That the hour has come, it has now arrived when the true worshipper shall worship the Father in Spirit and in Truth ... for the Father seeks for such to worship Him" (John 4:23–24). Biblical worship is meant to be an encounter with God in which one of the essential features is reality of faith and commitment, not outward form and ceremony. This relationship between inward reality and outward form must not, however, be seen in contrast but rather in complementary terms. It is unfortunate that this tension between spirit and form has often led Reformed church theologians and expositors to create an unbiblical dichotomy, or division, which is essentially Hellenistic in its understanding. "The spirit of the Old Testament is consistently not an order of spiritual being over against matter, but life giving creative activity pervading every aspect of life."[1]

As the New Testament is studied, there is also the realization that "in the worship of the New Covenant our response to the incarnate God does not reject sign and symbol, ceremony and sacrament."[2]

One verse that became particularly meaningful to the leaders of the Westminster Fellowship was found in Paul's First Letter to the Corinthians, when, after rebuking the believers in this

---

1. C.K. Barrett, *The Gospel According to St. John* (London: Society for the Publication of Christian Knowledge, 1972), p. 199.
2. Charles Davis, "Church Architecture and Liturgy" in R. Hammond, ed., *Toward a Church Architecture* (1962), p. 112.

church for their party spirit, the apostle encouraged them to realize that "all things are yours, whether Paul or Apollos, or Cephas, or the world, or life or death, or things present or things to come . . . all things are yours and you are Christ's and Christ is God's" (1 Cor. 3:21–23). This compelled the newly established congregation to see that it must not be rooted in biblical doctrine alone but must also affirm that the Church as a growing body must constantly reform itself in the light of Scripture. The congregation could not settle down as if it had discovered the ultimate word about worship and service. The sixteenth-century Reformation had rediscovered some of the great truths of Christianity, which had been minimized, distorted, and forgotten; but the Reformation had not rediscovered everything. While a sincere endeavor had been made to reform the life of the Church in the light of Scripture, it had neglected to express the fullness of the priesthood of all believers. This lack of relationship between the pastoral ministry and laity, which is seen so clearly in the New Testament witness, had curtailed the possible flow of the gifts of the Spirit, which Christ had given to his Church for its continuous upbuilding.

The discovery that in Christ "all things are ours" and that Christians must constantly be willing to be led by the Spirit reinforced the conviction that no one form of worship, either classical or contemporary, was binding on the Church for all time. This fact is expressed by Dr. Paul Hoon of Union Seminary.

The reality of Jesus Christ is to be grasped not under any single discrete aspect, but through all the meanings to which His Name and reality are attached. The fulness of the Word is like a spectrum of many colours and the Church has found itself liturgically beholden now by this doctrine and now by that. The resurrection and heavenly reign of Christ have distinctively claimed the devotion of Eastern Orthodoxy, incarnation and atonement in the piety of Roman Catholicism. Pentecostal worship characteristically stresses the Holy Spirit, the second coming and last judgment. Anglican liturgy emphasizes the doctrine of the incarnation. Up till recently much Protestant free worship has magnified the human and historical Jesus. Such diverse emphases in liturgy are surely to be welcomed. Indeed the fulness of the Word makes them inevitable.[3]

The Westminster Fellowship gradually realized the necessity to study the patterns of church life engaged in by Christians throughout the ages. The work of the Spirit had not ended with the closing of the apostolic age, as has been unfortunately expressed in some dispensational expositions of the Acts of the Apostles and 1 Corinthians. The Spirit is still at work, creating and incorporating into its life not only the historic foundational truths of apostolic Christianity but also the spiritual development of liturgy consistent with God's Word, as it has developed historically.

The Westminster Fellowship had often repeated the words of the Apostles' Creed, "I believe in the Holy Catholic Church." Now it was realized that this had to be a fact expressed in reality and not merely a traditional verbalization of something that had no practical meaning. This great creedal confession had to be incorporated into the liturgical worship of the services. It meant that there was a need to see the importance of the sacraments, especially a restoration of the Lord's Supper to the regular weekly observance seen in New Testament church life. The celebration of Christ's presence sacramentally had to be shared by the members of the congregation along with the pastoral ministers. The laity, the people of God, were invited to be involved in the act of consecration of the elements by offering the eucharistic prayers or prayers of thanksgiving.

The catholicity of the Church was also encouraged by studying other forms of worship with an openness to see how the Spirit was leading other Christian denominations. In this investigation forms of worship that the Fellowship knew would enrich our own services were discovered—the emphasis on quietness and reflection as stressed by the Quakers; the creative waiting upon God to unfold his Word from the members of the congregation, as understood by the Christian Brethren

---

3. Paul Hoon, *The Integrity of Worship* (Nashville and New York: Abingdon Press, 1971), p. 147.

(Plymouth); the joyous emphasis upon singing and praise, as practiced historically by Methodists and Baptists; the spirit of expectancy that the gifts of the Holy Spirit would operate, as grasped by the classical Pentecostals. The realization that the Church is a contemporary, living organism of Christ in the twentieth-century strengthened the intention of the Fellowship to be open to fresh approaches to worship that are being designed by liturgists today.

This sense of catholicity was linked to a deep feeling that sectarianism in all of its blatant and subtle forms is contrary to Christ's pattern for his people. In the light of this, the Fellowship endeavored to belong to those interdenominational ecumenical bodies that attempt to express the unity of the Body of Christ in our time. There was a growing realization of the truth expressed in Charles Davis's evaluation that "one of the results of the liturgical movement has been to bring Christians of different communions closer together, because the new understanding of liturgy is overcoming various distorting prejudices and defective ideas which all communions of the West have inherited from the Middle Ages and which explain in part, their divisions."[4]

As a congregation of Christians in the Reformed tradition, many of the members had begun to realize that the gifts of the Holy Spirit must be a functioning reality, and this linked them to the charismatic renewal that was taking place in the Presbyterian church, as well as in all the other churches of our day. However, they did not feel that the fresh realization of the Spirit's presence in their congregational and personal life had to be expressed in classical Pentecostal terms, nor were they obligated to bind the Fellowship to certain forms of worship that were acceptable to Pentecostals. For example, the Fellowship did not feel it was absolutely necessary for the Spirit to manifest all the gifts when they gathered for worship. The gathering of Christians for worship was not in order to speak in tongues, to prophecy, or to pray for miracles and healing. The purpose of worship is to be drawn to God through Jesus Christ,

---

4. Davis, "Church Architecture and Liturgy," p. 112.

acknowledging the sovereignty of his Spirit. They learned to wait for him to call forth the gifts of his Spirit as he willed. Services were not judged as a success or failure on the basis of outward manifestations of these gifts of power and edification. What is needed is encouragement of people to worship in a spirit of openhearted expectancy, taking seriously the Spirit's willingness to build up the Body of Christ. As teaching was given with respect to the relevance of the spiritual gifts, church members began to exercise faith and permitted the Spirit to operate through them in gift ministry. The Fellowship began to take seriously the words of R.C.D. Jasper in the *Renewal of Worship*: "It is heartening to realize at a time when Christians are perhaps more aware of the tragic estrangement of the world from the Church more than ever before, God is so plainly calling us to rediscover together the joy, the depth, the power of Christian worship."[5]

From the very beginning of the Westminster Fellowship's existence, the Spirit made it clear that worship in spirit and truth leads to loving witness to others and Christian acts of mercy. The discovery was made that whenever a congregation is excited about its worship of God and what he is doing in their lives through worship, then effective witness becomes a spontaneous, normal part of Christian living. Because the members of the Fellowship became excited about the reality of Christian worship, they could not help sharing this with their friends, business associates, and family. As a result, people whose lives were uncommitted began to attend the services, and many of them responded to the gospel. Concern for the spiritual well-being of others was a natural part of being rejuvenated in worship. This renewal of personal witness also increased interest in the worldwide mission of Christ. Many who had been nearsighted in their view of the world began to be concerned about the evangelization of their fellowman.

Worship and witness, however, were not seen as climactic to vital Christian living. Through biblical research, members of

---

5. Ronald C.D. Jasper, ed. *The Renewal of Worship* (New York, Toronto: Oxford University Press, 1965), p. 6.

the Fellowship saw afresh how much God cares for the downtrodden in society, the outcasts, the neglected misfits, the economically deprived, and the forgotten of the earth. God quickened to the hearts of the people the words of Isaiah 1:1–15, where the prophet makes it clear that God will not accept worship, prayer, and other ceremonies expressive of piety if there is a neglect of the fatherless, the widow, or those who stand in need of justice or deliverance from oppression. When we come to grips with our neglect of these people, then God addresses us, "Come, let us reason together, though your sins be as scarlet, they shall be as white as snow, though they be red like crimson they shall be as wool" (Isa. 1:18). These words were burned into their hearts by the Spirit, along with the teaching of Jesus that when Christians serve those who are in need, he is being served in a very direct and personal way (Matt. 25:31–46).

The realization of these facts surrounding the need for social compassion delivered the worship services from pietistic sentimentalism, creating a dynamic love that longed to be of help to men and women in every walk of life. Various members of the Fellowship became involved in a strong program of prison visitation, service to the retarded and the alcoholic, and child care through World Vision. In the services people felt free to express their own needs; and concerned attempts were made to help those in economic straits and those who were struggling with marital conflict, personal loss, sickness, and death. The Spirit enabled the Fellowship to see that worship that does not issue in strong social action motivated by love becomes a form of religious hypocrisy not according to truth. Worship loses its significance if it does not issue in the works of the Father done in the Spirit of Jesus.

The Bible was used by God to call the members of the Fellowship to a "doing of the truth," to a "love of neighbor as ourselves," to an expression of love in "deed and truth" as well as in words. Worship and witness become distorted and empty of reality if actions do not accompany these aspects of Christian service. There must be a vital identification of the Christian life with every form of human need. Thus the Church was seen not as a worshiping body alone but as one that must express its life in mission, guided by biblical insights. The Church is called to

7

serve, and this is the highest form of liturgical involvement. Christians gather and disperse. In our gatherings we acknowledge the reality of the God who has redeemed us in Christ, and we respond in joyous homage. In the services of worship we are meant to receive the power of the Spirit afresh, so that in our witness and acts of Christian love we can demonstrate the reality of faith in the One we worship.

As the Westminster Fellowship grew and developed in these areas, there was the realization that they were not a perfect church. They were in constant need of rediscovering what God wanted them to learn. They realized that while the kingdom of God was in their midst, it has not arrived in all its fullness. Therefore, along with all Christians, there must be a longing for the day when the worship and service, which are being offered to God in the glory of heaven by saints and angels, will eventually come to earth and fulfill the longing, "Thy Kingdom come, on earth, as it is in heaven."

# Chapter 1. Biblical Worship in the New Testament: Exposition of John 4:23–24

THE WORSHIP OF THE Christian Church is based upon two elements: the witness of the New Testament; and the types of worship that have developed throughout the centuries, a few as a direct result of the Spirit's leading and others based upon a human response to the contemporary situation.

When the Westminster Fellowship came into existence, it was deeply aware that the Lord was seeking to renew the life of the congregation in depth. The discoveries that were made in relation to the essential elements of worship were not made immediately. But as the Word of God was opened and serious attention was given to the significance of biblical patterns, a number of important developments began to take place. They entered into a deep realization that worship must be a central part of a Christian's life and of the importance of being open to the leading of the Spirit. There had to be as much freedom as possible from preconceived notions as to the nature of worship.

The leaders began to examine every text in Scripture that had anything to say about the subject of worship. This was an exciting adventure into an area where there was considerable limitation of understanding. A real urgency was felt to trust the Holy Spirit to reveal what it meant to "love the Lord our God, with all your heart, and with all your soul, and with all your mind, and with all your strength" (Mark 12:30). The Bible is full of instruction on the nature of worship, providing plenty of insight into how the ancient Israelites worshiped in Old Testament times and how the early Church developed patterns of worship (which were based upon experiences from the past) and the new dynamic move of the Spirit among them in the present.

The statement that began to challenge the thinking of members of the Westminster Fellowship was made by Jesus to the woman at the well of Sychar, recorded in John 4:23–24. In this conversation with the Samaritan woman, Jesus replied to her question on the locality of divinely appointed worship. "Our fathers worshipped in this mountain, and you say that in Jerusalem is the place where men ought to worship" (4:20). It was obviously a question designed to divert attention away from her sin and need for personal forgiveness and redemption. Jesus, nevertheless, immediately responded to her superficial remarks by giving her insights into the nature of true worship. He assured her that "the hour had come, and now is, when the true worshipper shall worship the Father in spirit and in truth for the Father seeks for such to worship Him. God is a Spirit, and they who worship him must worship him in spirit and in truth" (4:23–24). He did not intend this statement to be understood as propositional theological dogma, but rather as a dynamic response that could lead her into a living relationship with the God who would respond in love if her worship was "in spirit and in truth."

If the Church is going to experience the reality of renewal as a constant factor in its relationship with God, then there must be not only a desire to understand intellectually what it means to worship in spirit and in truth but also the realization of what it means to apply the truth to concrete forms of worship, which have developed in the life of the Church historically, being expressed today in the many churches that exist throughout the world.

John 4:23–24 is full of meaning with which the Church must constantly grapple in terms of her worship of God. The former Archbishop of Canterbury, William Temple, is right when he states, "It is the most fundamental proposition in theology."[1]

---

1. William Temple, *Readings in St. John's Gospel* (London: Macmillan & Co., 1939), p. 64.

Even though the Bible is full of passages that deal with the primacy of worship in the believer's life, "this statement is outstanding and almost unique in its affirmation both of the nature and of the true worship of God."[2]

These words of Jesus bring to our attention a few important facts that are of great significance for us, as they were for the woman at the well.

1. God is Spirit
2. God is deserving of worship
3. Worship must be offered to him in (a) spirit and (b) truth

## God Is Spirit

The reason why men are to worship God "in spirit and in truth" is because of who he is. Although Jesus did not attempt to define the nature of God on this occasion or to say many of the things that are said about him in Scripture, he did assert the spiritual nature of his Father when he declared, "God is Spirit."

It is important to emphasize at the outset that God is not *a* Spirit. "He is not just one of the beings that inhabit the spirit world. . . . He is not just one member of a clan of spirits."[3] All the commentators who write on this passage agree that this is not an attempt on the part of Jesus to present either a simple or profound definition of God for this woman's consideration. It was not important at this point in her life for her to understand the Hebrew meaning of the word *spirit*. These words were not given as a definition of God, even though that might appear to be so on the surface. Rather, "it is a metaphor of His mode of operation, as Life Giving power."[4] "It is not meant to be taken literally any more than God is Light (1 John 1:5) or that God is

2. John Marshall, *The Gospel of St. John* (Baltimore: Penguin Books, 1968), p. 220.

3. G.A. Turner and J.R. Mantey, *The Gospel According to John* (Grand Rapids: William B. Eerdman's, no date), p. 117.

4. Ibid.

a consuming fire (Heb. 12:29)."[5] This insight is strengthened by no less a scholar than Rudolf Bultmann, who comments, "This is not a definition in the Greek sense. It is not, that is, a mode of being proper to God as He is in Himself, by referring to it as Spirit."[6]

We will be greatly helped in our worship of God today if we understand what the Old Testament means when it speaks of God as "spirit." The word that is used in the Hebrew is "ruach" (רוח), or "pneuma" (πνεῦμα) in the Greek. The Septuagint, which is the Greek version of the Hebrew Old Testament, uses the term no less than 264 times. In all three places it refers to (a) breath, (b) wind, and (c) spirit. In several biblical passages it refers to the breath of one's mouth (Ps. 33:6, Job 19:17, 9:18, Jer. 12:34). But above all it is the breath of life that proceeds from God, both physical and spiritual.

Through the medium of wind God expresses his nature, which is so suggestive of his power and presence. Just as the wind can blow as a soft breeze; as the strong wind of a violent storm; as a hurricane; as a hot, dry blast from the desert; so God expresses himself in the variety of his own personality. The essential thing about the wind is that it is beyond man's control. Jesus referred to this characteristic of the wind when he said to Nicodemus in his nocturnal visit, "the wind blows where it wills and you hear its sound, but you cannot tell where it comes from or where it goes to" (John 3:8). The divine power, or wind of God, active in creation, is responsible for the physical life of man; his mental abilities (Deut. 34:9); his artistic sense (Ex. 31:3); it is the source of all religious fervor. In short, it is the vital force behind all living things.

Since God is the personal, creative power behind all things, this excludes any belief in so-called divine powers along the lines of "pantheistic, mythical-mystical understanding of the cosmos and the natural events. There are no immanent divine

---

5. J.N. Sanders and B.A. Mantey, *A Commentary on the Gospel According to St. John* (New York: Harper and Row, 1968), p. 1947.

6. Rudolf Bultmann, *The Gospel of John* (Philadelphia: The Westminster Press, 1971), p. 190.

forces in nature, which was so characteristic of the beliefs of people who surrounded the Hebrews."[7]

The same truth is expressed by William Temple, "God as Spirit is not to be understood in a pantheistic way as set forth in the teachings of Hinduism. God is a transcendent Spirit and not to be identified with Nature."[8] The wind is suggestive of the unfathomable mystery of God, who, although his divine dynamism can be discerned and experienced, is nevertheless unsearchable.

It is important to understand this truth as it relates to man and his origin in God. There are some religious theories that attempt to identify the nature of God with that of man. But the Bible makes it abundantly clear that "the Spirit of God is no natural quality of man. It is no hidden recess within our bodies."[9] The Hebrews did not divide the life of man into compartments and dimensions. They understood life in a total sense, in which God is at work in all things but not identical with everything. When God places his "ruach-spirit" in man, it is not something that is a private possession but rather, a power, a quality that is loaned him from God.

Thus the Spirit of God witnesses to God's sovereignty, something that cannot be controlled by man. God alone is the source of all life, manifesting himself in a variety of ways, depending upon the situation and the need. To describe God as Spirit is to reject the idolatry that is characteristic of many of man's religions. The pagan view of God, with its emphasis on the material, is obviously rejected, although idolatry must not be construed to be a simple concept that the more enlightened minds of our age have rejected. Idolatry manifests itself in the total life of man, and there is no area of our existence that is free from it. The philosophical concept of God as Spirit, as held

7. Gerhardt Friedrich, ed., *The Theological Dictionary of the New Testament* (Grand Rapids: William B. Eerdman's, 1968), pp. 359–362.
8. William Temple, *Readings in St. John's Gospel* (London: Macmillan & Co., 1939), p. 64.
9. Michael Green, *I Believe in the Holy Spirit* (Grand Rapids: William B. Eerdman's, 1975), p. 18.

by the later Greek philosophers, was understood as something in contrast to material substance, which was viewed as evil. But the Hebrew concept of God as Spirit did not allow for this distinction. God as the Creator of all things, both physical and spiritual, has declared the goodness of all things (Gen. 1). "God in the Old Testament is regularly not an order over against matter, but life giving creative power, and it is in this sense that it is used in John 4:24."[10]

Belief in God as Spirit is, therefore, something very radical, and linked with the self-revelation of God to man. With his natural mind, even though fallen and perverted, man can discern some aspects of the spiritual nature of life (Rom. 1:19-23). But we must not imagine that this insight makes man a possessor of the truth. In our present-day Western culture, we often take it for granted that everyone understands that God is spirit in his essential nature, but the actual fact is "that slowly do we learn that God is Spirit."[11] If we really believed that God is Spirit, we would not be so literalistic in our discussion of him or demand that he prove his reality in some material, visible way.

### God Is Worthy of Worship

The worship of God is one of the foundational truths of the Hebrew–Christian faith. What does the Bible mean when it calls upon man to worship God? In its original form, this word referred to the ancient custom of falling down before a person and kissing his feet, the hem of his garment, or the ground in front of the person being worshiped. Its Greek origin is *pros* (toward) or πρός and *kunew* (to kiss) or κυνέω. This is the most frequent use of the word in the New Testament and the one which Jesus used when speaking to the woman at the well. Paul used the word when he told the Corinthians that if a person

---

10. Marcus Dods, *The Gospel of St. John* (New York: A.C. Armstrong and Co., 1903), p. 153.
11. Ibid.

enters their congregation and hears a prophetic utterance, "the secrets of his heart will be revealed and he will fall down on his face and worship God" (1 Cor. 14:25). This bodily position meant to indicate the inner heart reaction to God when a person comes to worship him.

Nowhere in Scripture is worship clearly defined. Any consideration of the various passages of the Bible will show that worship is not confined to a mere verbal description alone. Broadly speaking, worship is something that occurs as a result of "direct acknowledgment of God, His nature, attributes, claims, whether it proceeds from a heart of praise, or by deeds which are done in grateful recognition of what God has done for the worshipper."[12] When we deal with the word as it is used in John 4:23–24, we must ask whether Jesus was insisting upon an act of worship that was accompanied by some outward expression, such as the word in its original meaning indicates (bowing down, falling down, kissing). Most commentators do not feel that Jesus is laying down any formal pattern of worship but, rather, is emphasizing the inner need for reality as we approach God with a heart yielded to him in obedience. But because Jesus was Hebraic in his understanding of God, he did not rule out the possibility of worship being expressed with bodily action, although he did not indicate what form that bodily action should take. Whatever is done must come from the heart and not be an empty liturgical act with no inner substance to it.

Much has been written on the subject of worship, but one of the finest studies has been done by Dr. Ralph Martin in his book *Worship in the Early Church*. Martin sums up all that the Bible says about the origin and nature of worship. "Worship then, is an intimate experience in which a grateful servant offers praise to His well-deserving master."[13] It involves service "which is not empty ritual, but a vital, living expression of

---

12. W.E. Vine, ed., *An Expositionary Dictionary of the New Testament Words* (Old Tappan, New Jersey: Fleming and Revell Co., 1940), pp. 233–234.

13. Ralph Martin, *Worship in the Early Church* (Grand Rapids: William B. Eerdman's and Co., 1964), p. 12.

gratitude for all that God is, and for all that He does."[14] Jesus was trying to help the woman at the well understand that worship is a response to God in terms of all that he is and all that he has done. When he says that we "must" worship in spirit and in truth, he is not claiming that God forces us to worship him. On the contrary, the reason men are to worship him is because they have discovered through his action in their lives that he is the living God, who has dealt with us in grace and love. Human sinfulness blinds us to the reality of God. To approach the God of the Bible is to discover how far short we have fallen from his glory. He cannot be approached flippantly, even though he desires his children to have an intimate relationship with him. The gracious character of God in his attitude toward sinners is what makes the biblical revelation absolutely unique in its understanding of the nature of God. It is possible for us to worship the almighty God because he has dealt with us graciously (Ps. 103). "Our worship is not in servile fear but in filial reverence which leads us to holy boldness and adoring love, but which never forgets who God is and what we are in His sight."[15]

To worship in spirit and truth is to grasp the revelation of who God is and what he has done. Those in Israel who believed in the grace of God, which was extended to them as a nation in their miraculous deliverance from Egypt, became aware of his forgiveness of their sins through the symbolism of the sacrificial system. This knowledge of God finds its ultimate climactic revelation in Jesus Christ. Because of our discovery of him through the work of the Spirit in our hearts, "this is sufficient to call forth loudest and most triumphant chords of worship and praise. Christian worship finds its true center and its main inspiration as it declares the mighty acts of redemption in Christ."[16]

---

14. Ibid.
15. Ibid., p. 15.
16. Ibid.

## God Is to Be Worshiped in (a) Spirit and (b) Truth

When our Lord addressed himself briefly, and yet ever so pointedly, to the woman who asked the question about "where" to worship, he went to the heart of the question by indicating that a new age had dawned, in which the outward place did not matter as it had in the past. The new age had come, indeed, it has arrived permanently (John 4:23). What really mattered was man's inward spirit and attitude, free from hypocrisy and lifeless formality. The terms "in spirit and in truth" are used by John to bring out the fact that "the eschatological age has been brought about by Jesus . . ., those who worship in the spirit are those who have been born of the Spirit."[17]

Jesus knew that the Samaritans worshiped at Mt. Gerizim at their sacred shrine, with their limited understanding of God (John 4:22). He also knew that the Jews worshiped at Jerusalem in the Temple, with a true knowledge of God as the author of man's salvation (John 4:22). But as yet neither Samaritans nor Jews had a full grasp of the nature of spiritual worship, which he was to initiate. Only as men entered into an understanding of who he was could they truly worship God in spirit. "The Spirit is God's miraculous dealing with men, which takes place only in revelation."[18] To worship spiritually one must be filled with the Holy Spirit, an experience that was yet to come when the resurrection had taken place and the Spirit had been poured out on Pentecost. It was as a result of these events that believers would be able to worship God in spirit, not bound by geographical circumstances. In his commentary on John, the great nineteenth-century preacher and expositor, Dr. Campbell Morgan writes, "It is not a question of locality of worship. Moreover it is not a question of intellect merely. To worship, men must get down to the deepest thing in their personality, spirit and truth. There must be honesty. There must be reality.

---

17. Bultmann, *The Gospel of John*, p. 190.
18. Ibid.

17

Gerizim is nothing. Jerusalem is nothing. Spirit and truth is everything."[19]

The emphasis that had been placed by both Jews and Samaritans on location was being set aside by Jesus as irrelevant. Worship occurs wherever the human heart has been brought into a right relationship with God through repentance and faith. Thus Jesus emphasized that "whether one worships at this place or that place, worship must operate in the realm of spirit and truth."[20]

This was the conviction of all the sixteenth-century Reformers and their successors in the classical Protestant tradition. Many commentators could be quoted, but the great Anglican theologian R.H. Lightfoot sums them all up when he writes, "Our Lord rules out the problem of [place] as no longer relevant. Very soon the day of local and differing, as opposed to universal and united, worship is to pass. Indeed the hour of the new worship is already come. It is a worship which is no longer to be offered by the non-Jews in their ignorance (Acts 17:25) or in accordance with Jewish rites."[21] God is not to be worshiped according to pagan ideas created by men all over the world and expressed in idolatrous religious devotion to material objects, for "God is not a stone deity, or a tree deity, or a mountain deity, so as to be worshiped on this or that mountain. He is independent, a personal being, truly alive, and worthy of worship that is real."[22]

The worship that was part of the Jewish life under the Mosaic dispensation and in the Samaritan heresy is no longer a necessary part of true worship. True worshipers are those who recognize that something radically different has been brought into operation, namely, worship that is spiritual in character.

---

19. Campbell Morgan, *The Gospel According to John* (New York: Fleming and Revell Co. date unknown), pp. 76–77.

20. William Hendriksen, *Exposition of the Gospel According to John* (Grand Rapids: Baker Publishing House, 1953), p. 167.

21. R.H. Lightfoot, *St. John's Gospel* (Oxford at the Claredon Press, 1956), p. 124.

22. Hendriksen, *Gospel According to John*, p. 168.

This radical change has come about because of the revelation of God in Jesus and not because men have reasoned their way to a new approach. This is seen by C.K. Barrett, who writes, "True worshipers realize that all that was foreshadowed but not fulfilled in the worship of the Jews at Jerusalem and by the Samaritans at Mt. Gerizim, is not because a higher level of worship has been reached in the course of man's development in which the material side of holy places can be dispensed with, but because Jesus Himself is the true fulfillment of God's purpose and thus the anticipation of the future worship of God."[23] The emphasis which Jesus placed upon worship was not in terms of race or place but in terms of spirit and truth. These are the two key words that are necessary for our understanding today if our worship is to be in accordance with God's plan for his children.

## Spiritual Worship

The word *spirit* in New Testament thinking refers to that which is nonmaterial; and yet it is linked to the material, because it is linked to man and those things which men have used to worship him. The worship of God in the Old Testament was intensely spiritual. And yet it was expressed through material objects, such as the tabernacle and all its furniture; the temple and its ritual ceremonies; through such acts as the reading of Scripture, the offering of spoken prayer, the singing of praise, the playing of instruments, and the wearing of liturgical dress. To think of worship as spiritual does not necessarily rule out the use of some or all of these things.

In the conversation that Jesus had with the Jewish ruler Nicodemus (John 3), our Lord referred to the phenomenon of wind as a symbol of God's activity in man's life. Nicodemus was familiar with the idea because of his Hebrew background, but it is obvious that he had not grasped its significance (John 3:9). As

23. C.K. Barrett, *The Gospel According to John* (London: Society for the Publication of Christian Knowledge, 1972), p. 199.

we have already seen from our consideration of "ruach" in the Old Testament, wind is a sign of God's sovereign presence, which cannot be controlled or manipulated by men. Just as the wind cannot be brought under man's control, so the Spirit of God cannot be forced into any particular mold by man's will. It is so important for our understanding of worship to realize that the wind points to God's action. The wind cannot be controlled, and neither can God be brought under man's management. The wind blows where it wishes, and we hear the sound and see the effects, but we cannot tell where it comes from or where it goes (John 3:8). The wind, with all of its variety, is so suggestive of God's action when men gather for worship. The expression of worship must be submitted to the control of God's Spirit, and he will express his reality to us in a variety of ways and forms. He operates within the laws which he has created, and yet he is not bound by any of them. He is able to move over and beyond them in the outworking of his purpose, and all of this is particularly true when we apply it to the reality of worship.

When we respond to God in worship activated by the Spirit and governed by his truth, Jesus is clear in his teaching to the woman at the well that this is what God wants in our worship. But this kind of spiritual, truth-informed worship comes about only when the spirit of man is regenerated by the Spirit of God. This is why Jesus was so insistent in his conversation with Nicodemus that there must be a spiritual rebirth. In our natural unregenerated minds we may have some concept of what we think it means to worship deity. But it is only when we are born anew from within by the Spirit of God that man is able to worship in accordance with Jesus' teaching—in spirit and in truth. When the Holy Spirit activates the spirit of the Christian, the first thing he does is worship. We see this from the passage in Acts 2. On the day of Pentecost, the apostles were so filled with the Spirit that they caused a great stir in Jerusalem by the intensity of the worship they offered God. We must not see this action of the Spirit simply in terms of external manifestations, such as wind, tongues of fire, and the utterance of "Spirit language." What is more important is that the words of Jesus were being fulfilled in them: "Out of your innermost being shall flow rivers of living water" (John 7:38). With the exaltation of Jesus, this new, spiritual worship could be offered to God. Thus the words of Jesus to the Samaritan woman were prophetic in nature because they pointed to the time when they would be fulfilled in the full release of the Spirit's presence. As far as Jesus himself was concerned, spiritual worship was already a reality, for that was the kind of relationship he had continually with his Father. The dimensions of truth in the spirit operated in him fully. The day would come when his disciples would also share in the same depths of worship as he did.

Although the spiritual relationship between a believer and God must be as Father and son, the spirituality of worship is not something that remains unchanged. Not even when the Spirit's gifts are operating in the local church do we always see a manifestation of worship in spirit and in truth. Paul commended the Corinthians for not lagging behind in the manifestations of gifts, yet he was compelled to speak to them as "babes" because of their immature spirituality, which expressed itself in disorderly worship (1 Cor. 14). If the Christian does not live under the control of the Spirit, he may express a spirituality that is characterized by jealousy and a party spirit. Even if he engages in the kind of spiritual worship described in 1 Corinthians 14:26, he may still be a spiritual baby in his behavior. The state of mind necessary for worship in "spirit and in truth" must be governed by a yieldedness to the word of God or to the truth, with a constant submission to God's judgments. Those who are spiritual in worship must be willing to be led by the Spirit in terms of his truth concerning conduct and attitudes. True spirituality is not a fixed, absolute condition. It requires growth, and this development is related to a constant increase of fellowship with Jesus Christ, the Truth. As we grow in our knowledge of him, the spirituality of our worship will be in evidence.

To worship in "spirit" is therefore a result of "being in the Spirit" (Rev. 1:10). It is not some vague, mystical condition, which may say all the right words but be lacking in reality. Some forms of Christian worship are perfectly orthodox (in the truth) as far as theological content is concerned but lifeless because there is no dependence upon the Spirit to activate true worship into existence. If a person is to worship in "spirit," he must be spiritually renewed and indwelt by the Spirit. He must be growing in the knowledge of the reality of Jesus Christ, which is growth in the truth. There must be a constant hungering for God, which is characteristic of all those who have truly sought after him with all their hearts (Ps. 42).

It is interesting to note that John, in his record of the conversation between Jesus and the Samaritan woman, relates the woman's desire for "water which causes her never to thirst again," which indicates her deeper need to be delivered from her sin and given power to worship from the depths of her being. She came to the well seeking water. But the Lord, through his request for a drink of the natural water, awakened in her a desire for something more. When she told him that she wanted the "water" he was offering her, she did not grasp the significance of her words. She did not realize that just as the body needs water to assuage its thirst, so the spirit of man needs the true knowledge of God to survive.

There is an aspect of worshiping in spirit and in truth that has often been misunderstood, even by the Reforming fathers, who were used by God to initiate a new call to spiritual worship which had been lacking in the Church for centuries. The medieval Church had corrupted the gospel by the creation of a maze of ceremonies and rituals that hid the reality of that gospel. The Reformers, because of their openness to the truth of God's Word, reacted against this kind of spirituality, and rightfully so. Nevertheless, though the Reformers realized that spiritual worship comes from within the life of the believer, directed toward God with a due sense of reality, they did not appreciate the relationship between those things which we call physical or material and the way God works through these outward things to produce spiritual worship.

The word *spirit*, as we have seen so far, does not rule out the material world. Indeed, God has often worked by his Spirit through material things. Spirit refers to that which is creative, alive, meaningful, and not necessarily nonmaterial. The Reformers, in reacting against the worship of the Church in their day, went a little too far in their denunciations. They tended to feel that spiritual worship was unassociated with anything that was material or formal.

But this was not what Jesus was saying when he insisted that only in spiritual reality are men involved in the worship of God. The kind of interpretation expressed by the Reformers and many of their successors is dangerously close to heresy, because it fails to perceive the Old Testament concept of what it means to be spiritual. In Hebrew thought there is no contrast between spirit and material. Both are created by God and meant to be under his control. Both are mediums through which his Spirit expresses his reality. Worship in the tabernacle and temple were not unspiritual because they both used forms and ceremonies. When Jesus speaks of worshiping in spirit, "he is not contrasting external worship with internal worship. His statement has nothing to do with worshiping God within the inner recesses of one's own spirit."[24] We must remember that the forms and ceremonies used in the Old Testament worship were instituted by God; and while they were to be superseded by a deeper form of worship in the New Age, which Jesus came to inaugurate, they are not to be seen as worship patterns antagonistic to his Spirit. These ceremonies only became obstacles to the essence of true worship and the object of the denunciations of the prophets (Isa. 1) when they were given an exaggerated importance and made into substitutes for the reality of God himself.

The Reformers had seen so much of this type of perversion in the worship of the medieval Church that they felt perfectly in order in denouncing it, even as the prophets had repudiated the unspiritual worship of the Israelites. They were right in wanting to cleanse the Church from superstitious rites, which had been introduced into the services over the years. But Calvin is partially blind to the situation when he writes, "What it is to worship God in spirit and in truth appears plainly from what has been said already . . . it is to remove the coverings from the

---

24. Raymond Brown, *The Gospel According to John* (Garden City, New York: Doubleday & Co., 1966), p. 180.

ancient ceremonies and retain what is spiritual in the worship of God. For the truth of the worship of God rests in the spirit, and ceremonies are so to say, adventious."[25] Again he comments, "Why and in what sense is the worship of God to be called spiritual? To understand this we must note the antithesis between Spirit and the external figures, as between shadow and substance. The worship of God is said to consist in the Spirit because it is only the inward faith of the heart that produces prayer and purity of conscience and denial of ourselves that we may be given up to the obedience of God as holy sacrifices."[26]

Calvin's teaching on the spirituality of worship influenced the succeeding generations of Reformed theologians and pastors up until modern times. The outward forms of worship were reduced to nothing in the desire to elevate what they understood to be the spiritual and nonceremonial character of worship. "For however the Lord did require and was pleased with these external forms in the infancy of the Church, yet He never did accept any of them."[27] This is not exactly true, because God did institute the worship of the tabernacle and did it according to a divine plan, even though it was intended to be temporary. The general attitude of Reformed Christians has been one of hostility toward anything that is suggestive of pomp and ceremony. The emphasis has been on simplicity and not "carnal shadows." But though this attitude has changed considerably in modern times, the exaggerated position of the Reformers was taken to extremes by some Christians, such as the Quakers, who rejected totally any outward signs or symbols of faith, all rites and ceremonies—even to denying the validity of the two New Testament sacraments of baptism and the Lord's Supper.

It is unfortunate that the Reformers did not spell out more clearly what they meant by the word *spiritual*. For them it

---

25. John Calvin, *Commentary on the Gospel of St. John* (Grand Rapids: William B. Eerdman's, 1959), p. 101.

26. Ibid., p. 99.

27. George Hutchinson, *An Exposition of the Gospel According to St. John* (Grand Rapids: Kregel Publications, 1959), p. 64.

usually meant "simple, reverent, anything which quickened humility."[28] And in defining it in this way they sought to undergird the need for sincere inner response to God. But "an ideal of purely internal worship ill befits the New Testament sense with its eucharistic gatherings, hymn singing, baptism in water, unless one assumes that John's theology is markedly different from that of the Church at large."[29] The Reformation certainly did not free itself from these forms, because there was a real attempt to be faithful to the Scriptures of the New Testament. There has always been the use of the Bible, preaching, singing, verbal prayer, and the sacraments. All these have been used in public worship. All these forms may degenerate into mere formalism unless activated into life by the power of the Spirit. Spiritual worship does not mean noninvolvement with material things or bodily action. It is, rather, permitting the Spirit to activate all our forms so that they become mediums through which God may reveal himself. Our understanding of the word *spirit* must not lead us to reject outward forms any more than believing that the Christian man who is spiritually minded should lead us to deny the significance of his physical body. It is a known fact that the Church in its expansion into the Greco-Roman world fell under the spell of Greek philosophy and made the tragic mistake of denying the spirituality of the body. But this is not the way the Bible conceives the relationship between body and spirit, or spirit and material, or the outward and inward forms of religious worship.

Biblical scholarship reinforces the conviction that "in the Spirit" does not mean a repudiation of any outward acts through which the truth of God may be symbolized. Barnabas Lindar writes, "The contrast is not between forms and ceremonies of the temple and the spiritual worship of the church, but between worship which is apart from Jesus and worship within His filial relationship with the Father, such as He revealed in His Passion."[30] Again he states, "Although it is true that the

---

28. Ibid., p. 65.

29. Brown, *Gospel According to John*, p. 180.

30. Barnabas Lindar, *The Gospel of John* (London: Oliphants, Marshall and Organ and Scott, 1972), p. 189.

Church abandoned Jewish ceremonies and in common with many thoughtful people placed the emphasis upon the heart and mind there is no polemic against forms and ceremonies as such. The fact that true worship is set over against idolatry and over against a cult restricted to one sanctuary is not more than incidental. The fundamental thing is that the worship expresses a relationship between God and man. This has to be spiritual because God is Spirit and therefore man too must have the Spirit. This according to John's theology is precisely what has been established by Jesus."[31]

It is so important for us to realize, as we come to grips with the nature of charismatic worship, that the word *spirit* must not be interpreted as a vague spirituality or as something that Christians produce as they attempt to overcome the more material aspects of this earthly life. This approach was often taken by nineteenth-century liberalism, which not only denied some of the basic doctrines of the Christian faith but tended to reduce the essence of Christian spirituality to a religious feeling. This was seen primarily in the teachings of Freidrich Schleiermacher, who greatly influenced Protestant thinking in the nineteenth and early twentieth centuries. Even the great Scottish Bible teacher William Barkley, whose commentaries have been so helpful, errs in his understanding of the nature of spiritual worship.

> A man's spirit is the highest part of man. That is the part of him which lasts when the physical part of him has vanished. It is the spirit of man which is the source and origin of his highest dreams, thoughts, ideals and desires. The true, the genuine worship, is when man, through his spirit, attains to a friendship and intimacy with God. To worship is not to come to a certain place, it is not to go through a certain ritual or liturgy, it is not even to bring certain gifts. True worship is when in the spirit, the immortal and invisible parts of man, speaks to and meets with God who is immortal and invisible.[32]

---

31. Ibid., p. 190.

32. William Barkley, *The Gospel of John* (Philadelphia: The Westminster Press, 1956), p. 156.

This otherwise evangelical scholar has been unduly influenced by nineteenth-century liberalism and a kind of Hindu Vedantism, which makes no distinction between the spirit of man (which, according to the Bible, is alienated from God, Ephesians 2:1), and the Spirit of God. This is not the biblical understanding of man's spirit nor the essence of the teaching which Jesus brought to the woman at the well.

The basis of worship is not

> That of some of the nineteenth century writers, as if Christianity were free from everything that ties men to time, space and ceremonies. If the Gospel has a precise reference to the Spirit that descended and remained upon Jesus, then the evangelist is not writing of some subjective spirituality, but the Spirit of Christ acting in power to finish the divine work in Christ and through His Church. Christian worship in reality is worship in the Spirit, and is precisely tied down to those acts of God in Christ which constitute man's redemption. That is why the Christian religion is at once the most free and the most bound of all. Free in the freedom of the Spirit and bound to Scripture, to sacrament and preaching, to worship in His Name. True worship spirituality is not achieved by abstracting it from everything particular, concrete, and historical for the sake of that which is purely universal, abstract and a-temporal. Rather it is a grateful acceptance of a way into the truly Internal through the concrete historical life, death, resurrection and exaltation of Jesus Christ.[33]

One other biblical scholar who helps to correct the overcorrecting of the Reformers and some nineteenth-century liberals is E.C. Hoskyns, who affirms,

> The contrast between false and true worship does not lie therefore in a distinction between worship which is directed toward some visible and material object, and that which is abstracted from all contact with the visible world, nor does it lie in a distinction between sacrificial and nonsacrificial or inward

---

33. Marshall, *The Gospel of St. John*, p. 220.

worship. False worship is directed toward a visible object regarded as itself complete and final. True worship is directed toward the flesh and blood of Jesus Christ, because it is there that you will see the heavens opened.[34]

Although I have attempted to make the point that spiritual worship is not a rejection of formal rites and ceremonies such as have been used by the Church in both Old and New Testament periods, it is essential to state that spiritual worship is not dependent upon outward forms and symbolic acts in any absolute way. We must agree with Marcus Dodds, that "Christ is opposed to empty symbolic worship but also to ignorant worship. Worship is not just a matter of inward sincerity. No doubt many sincere people engage in the worship of their gods but their worship is not based upon God's revelation of Himself. For this reason forms can be inadequate and deceptive."[35] He then goes on to interpret what Jesus was attempting to help the Samaritan woman understand.

> The Jewish worship, the context of which Jesus was speaking to the woman, was a worship in which every person, every colour, every gesture, every movement had a meaning for the initiated. But the time for this, says our Lord, is past. They need no longer take an animal to the temple to symbolize that they gave themselves to God, they were to spend their whole care on the real thing, on giving themselves to God. They were not to set candles about their altars to show that light had come, but they were themselves to symbolize the sweet smelling prayers of the saints. They were to offer prayers from humble hearts. They were to grow up into full understanding and worship, not merely without outward signs of reality, but with Reality itself.[36]

---

34. E.C. Hoskyns, *The Fourth Gospel* (London: Faber and Faber, 1947), p. 151.

35. Dods, *The Gospel of St. John* (New York: A.C. Armstrong and Son, 1903), pp. 157–158.

36. Ibid.

# Chapter 1

Allen, G.A., and Mantey, J.R. *The Gospel According to John*. Grand Rapids: William B. Eerdman's, n.d.

Arndt, William F., and Gingrich, F. Wilbur. *Greek-English Lexicon of the New Testament*. Chicago: University of Chicago Press, 1962.

Barret, C.K. *The Gospel According to John*. London: Society for the Publication of Christian Knowledge, 1972.

Bultmann, Rudolf. *The Gospel of John*. Philadelphia: The Westminster Press, 1971.

Dods, Marcus. *The Gospel of St. John*. New York: A.C. Armstrong and Son, 1903.

Friedrich, Gerhardt, ed., tr. by Bromley, G.W. *Theological Dictionary of the New Testament*. Grand Rapids: William B. Eerdman's, 1968.

Green, Michael. *I Believe in the Holy Spirit*. Grand Rapids: William B. Eerdman's, 1975.

Harrison, Everett F., ed. *Baker's Dictionary of Theology*. 4th ed. Grand Rapids: Baker House, 1969.

Hendriksen, William. *Exposition of the Gospel According to John*. Grand Rapids: Baker Publishing House, 1953.

Hutchinson, George. *An Exposition of the Gospel According to St. John*. Grand Rapids: Kregel Publishing House, 1953.

Lightfoot, R.H. *St. John's Gospel*. Oxford at Claredon Press, 1956.

Marshall, John. *The Gospel of St. John*. Baltimore: Penguin Books, 1968.

Martin, Ralph. *Worship in the Early Church*. Grand Rapids: William B. Eerdman's, 1964.

Morgan, Campbell. *The Gospel According to John*. New York: Fleming and Revell, n.d.

Sanders, J.N., and Mantey, B.A. *The Gospel According to St. John*. New York: Harper & Row, 1968.

Temple, William. *Readings in John's Gospel*. London: Macmillan & Co., 1939.

Vine, W.E. ed., *An Expositionary Dictionary of New Testament Words*. Old Tappan, New Jersey: Fleming and Revell Co., 1940.

# Chapter 2. Important Aspects
# of Reformed Church Worship

## The Sixteenth Century Reforming Church

THE REFORMERS OF THE Protestant tradition are a source of inspiration to us for many reasons, the primary one being that they took a bold stand for what they believed concerned the gospel and the Word of God. It was this concern for truth which inspired the members of the Westminster Fellowship. Many of them felt deeply reformed in their faith because they had been forced into Bible study of those passages which had to do with the activity of the Holy Spirit, the nature of worship, and the place of the gifts of the Spirit in the life of the Church. They came to the conclusion that although their new experience of the Holy Spirit's power was not inconsistent with the Reformed church's teaching on that subject, they had moved a step forward in understanding a doctrine that has never been finalized by the Church.

The times of the Reformation were governed by a particular set of concerns, and the restoration of the gifts of the Spirit to their proper place in the worship of the Church was not one of the interests of the Reformers. It is possible that if the Reformers were living today, they might have rejected the classical Pentecostal understanding of the Baptism of the Holy Spirit, but they would have enthusiastically embraced the Pentecostal spirit in terms of worship. Michael Green, of St. John's College, Nottingham, in his recent book, *I Believe in the Holy Spirit*, expresses this conviction when he writes, "if they [the Reformers] had lived in our day . . . they would have retained the biblical sense of the Word as the divine element in Christian initiation, but they would want to go all the way with the Pentecostals in emphasizing the deep experience of God."[1] The true spirit of the Reformation was not one of static conformity but, rather, an openness to constant reformation. The tension between the times in which they lived, with its particular need for innovation, in the light of the supremacy of the Word of God in all matters of faith and practice, was a continual problem confronting them. Calvin wrote in his Institutes, "Because God did not will in outward discipline and ceremonies to prescribe in detail all that we ought to do, because He foresaw that this depended upon the state of the times and he did not deem one form suitable for all ages."[2] The Reformers were part of a radical movement of renewal, and yet at the same time, they were not trying to create a new church or to indulge in innovation in order to appear original or creative. The spirit of Reformation was expressed by Calvin in these words, "I indeed admit that we ought not to charge into innovation rashly, suddenly, or for insufficient cause. But above all we will best judge the way we may hurt or edify, and if we let love be our guide, we will be sure."[3]

The desire to conform to the Word of God was the highest concern of the Reforming fathers. This attitude gripped the members of the Westminster Fellowship also. They knew that the Spirit is constantly at work, and while Christians may be committed to the great, unchanging doctrines of the biblical Christianity, there is a need to be open to new approaches to worship that are not inconsistent with the Word of God. These new forms, of course, must be an expression of the ultimate concern to be constantly under the lordship of Christ in all things that pertain to the worship of God. For this reason, the Westminster Fellowship felt justified in moving forward more

1. Michael Green, *I Believe in the Holy Spirit* (Grand Rapids: William B. Eerdman's, 1975), p. 147.

2. John Calvin, *The Institutes of the Christian Religion* (Philadelphia: The Westminster Press, 1959), Book 4, 10, 29, p. 1208.

3. Ibid.

than the Reformers did, because they sensed the Spirit leading in this direction. But this leading was not in terms of contemporary concerns alone but a desire to put into action what was being heard as the Scriptures were being studied with reference to the nature of worship.

One of the most important features of the Westminster Fellowship's relationship to the Presbyterian and Reformed tradition was that it did not see itself as a new church embarking upon "doing its own thing" for the sake of religious freedom. They felt tied to the whole Body of Christ, including the Reformed churches; and the primary concern was to be loyal to the Word of God, understanding their new experience "in the Holy Spirit" in terms of the Scriptures. They prayed constantly that the Spirit would guide them in a direction that would be greater conformity to the written word of God.

This was certainly the overarching desire of the Reformers of the sixteenth century, particularly those who were influenced by the teaching of John Calvin. Martin Luther gave leadership to the Reformation churches in Germany in such a way as to bring the gospel into proper focus again, but he did not change the order of the Mass greatly. Indeed, he felt that for the sake of the older people this would be an unwise step. Zwingli, however, had stripped the traditional worship of the medieval church of almost everything except the reading and preaching of the Word of God, along with the offering of prayers. But the singing of hymns and other liturgical forms were eliminated. It was Calvin who had a more radical, and yet balanced, expression of biblical worship than any other.

In understanding the worship that developed under the leadership of Calvin in Geneva, it is necessary to understand something of the times in which he lived, the struggles which engaged his attention, and the knowledge that he had of Scripture and tradition. Calvin's Geneva was made up of a large influx of people who had recovered the reality of the gospel but were suffering for their faith because of papal persecution against them in their particular countries. This tended to make them very critical of Rome, not only at the level of what they felt was the perversion of the gospel but also with certain practices that had become part of the embellishment of medieval worship. The great recovery of the Reformed church was the doctrine of justification by faith through grace. This doctrine was instrumental in giving the Reformed Christians a new sense of liberty, yet they were reluctant to go as far as the Anabaptists in their reformation of church worship and the Christian life. The Reformers were more inclined to a "liturgical policy based upon the warrant of Scripture and the custom of the Ancient Church."[4]

Although Calvin was not a literalist in his scriptural interpretation, he nevertheless felt bound to the Scriptures in determining what should be incorporated into the worship service. He did not attempt to fully recover the worship that was practiced in the original New Testament Church, but he did retain much of what he felt was the pattern of worship in the second and third centuries. However, his knowledge of what had taken place at the time was limited. James Hasting Nicols points out that the sixteenth century knew nothing of the Didache written around 100 A.D. or the Roman Order given in 225 A.D. by Hippolysus, or the Egyptian Prayer Book of Athanasius' friend Sarapion.[5] Furthermore, as we have already stated, the "Reformers were not those who supposed that somewhere there is a right liturgical form for Christian worship. The Reformers, especially Calvin, contended that Reformed worship was closer to that experienced by Gregory, Bazil, Chrysostrom, Augustine, Ambrose and Cyrian, than that of the 16th century Mass."[6]

We may criticize the Reformers for not being more faithful to the tradition of Scripture, accepting without biblical warrant some of the patterns established in the second and third centuries, which provided the basis for later Roman usage. But I feel that this criticism is blind to certain facts that emerge in the New Testament. Certainly the early Christians were not en-

---

4. Bard Thompson, *Liturgies of the Western Church* (New York: New American Library, 1961), p. 185.

5. James Hasting Nicols, *Corporate Worship in the Reformed Tradition* (Philadelphia: The Westminster Press, 1968), pp. 13–14.

6. Ibid., p. 14.

tirely free from Old Testament concepts, and no one can read the book of Acts without seeing that the early Christians were a community of Jewish believers in transition from Mosaic patterns to forms peculiarly Christian in content and expression. There is nothing in the New Testament to indicate that the early Christians abolished entirely everything that they had known from the past. The centrality of the Word of God was there, the singing of psalms and hymns, the sacramental fulfillment of the Passover in the Lord's Supper. To imagine that they stripped their services of everything that reminded them of their Jewish roots is not credible. This is supported by James Hasting Nicols, who writes,

> The church was at the same time organizing its own synagogue service of Biblical readings, praise, prayer, and preaching. In apostolic times Christians could count on the Jewish synagogue for these means of worship, at least for the Old Testament. Their own preaching rather was testimony to the gospel of Jesus by eyewitnesses, or from oral traditions, or as interpreted by "prophets" in the Spirit. But the growing rupture with the synagogue and the inevitable replacement of eyewitnesses and oral tradition with written gospels combined to lead the second-century church to devise a Christian practice of reading and exposition akin to that of the synagogue. When this Christian service of Scriptural exposition was joined to the "token" Lord's Supper, as had happened in Rome by about A.D. 150, from Justin's report, the basic pattern of Catholic worship was laid down. The Reformers simply took over this tradition and made no effort to go behind the second century to the pattern of the apostles.[7]

The first concern of Calvin was to exalt the majesty of God in worship, which was consistent with his revelation in Jesus Christ and the Word of God. No one could have been more committed to the centrality of worship in the life of the Christian than he. But he did recognize clearly that there was true and false worship. He writes, ". . . the first foundation of righteousness is the worship of God. When this is overthrown, all the remaining parts of righteousness, like the pieces of a

---

7. Ibid., p. 21.

34

shattered and fallen building, are mangled and scattered.
. . . Therefore we call the worship of God the beginning and foundation of righteousness. When it is removed, whatever equity, continence, or temperance men practice among themselves is in God's sight empty and worthless."[8] This is one of the reasons he felt so strongly that the service must be free from any ritual or observance that clouds the glory of the Gospel and the majesty of God. He frowned upon anything that he felt deflected from the simplicity of faith in Christ, causing worshipers to trust in some ritual observance rather than in the grace of God alone. This was certainly a healthy concern, and we can perfectly understand why he reacted against ritual the way he did.

However, anxiety often causes people to react in a much greater degree than they should, and this is one of our criticisms of Calvin. He tended to move too far to the extreme in his denunciations of anything that suggested form or ritual. He expressed his anxiety constantly in his writings, denouncing men who "improvise upon the Word though they toil much in outward rites are yet impious and contumacious, because they will not suffer themselves to be ruled by God's authority."[9] He encouraged the least possible admixture of human invention and felt that most attempts to retain formality only encouraged sin and vanity. Men can do nothing but err when they are guided by their own opinions. He felt that idolatry was fostered by those who "introduced newly invented methods of worshipping God which really adore and worship the creature of their own distempered imaginations."[10]

We may conclude from this that Calvin favored a "liturgy from which the ministers be not allowed to vary, for it curtailed the capricious giddiness and levity of such as effect innovations."[11] He condoned the use of ceremonies that "served decency, order and reverence, conceding the value to the stimulus and expression of religion. But in the main, he

---

8. Calvin, *The Institutes*, Book 2, p. 377.
9. Thompson, *Liturgies of the Western Church*, p. 194.
10. Ibid., p. 195.
11. Ibid.

crammed his writings with the damnation of lifeless and theatrical trifles and feared nothing more than that a floodgate of ceremonies would be opened."[12] It is unfortunate that his understanding of the word *spirit* led him to adopt a more Greek than Hebraic interpretation of spiritual worship, for as we have seen from our consideration of the word *spirit*, it does not mean that form, ritual, or ceremony are necessarily unspiritual in and of themselves. They can become unspiritual if we permit them to overpower the inner reality of what they are attempting to express. But unspiritual worship is not a matter of indulging in "ceremonial subterfuges."

Although Calvin and his followers did not want the church service to be dominated by ceremonial rites such as they saw in the medieval church, they did not want to develop a form of worship that was inflexible, governed according to strict predetermined patterns, such as a prayer book might require. They were not interested in preserving "artistic taste or priestly validities, but rather the integrity of service and devotion."[13] By integrity of devotion they had in mind a service that centered on the Word of God, which would be read and taught, responded to in song and prayer; and in the celebration of the Lord's Supper, which Calvin saw as one of the most important parts of the liturgy to be retained by the Church. It is the preaching of the Word that is of paramount importance for Christians. He therefore called the reading and preaching of the Word "the incomparable treasure of the Church."[14] The liturgy of the Word was twofold, made up of the reading of Scripture followed immediately by the sermon. Thus, the Scripture reading and preached Word were inseparable.[15] The reading and preaching of the Word, the one following upon the other, saved the service from being improperly divided, commonly characteristic of modern Protestantism, which needs to be re-

---

12. Ibid.
13. Nicols, *Corporate Worship*, p. 21.
14. Thompson, *Liturgies of the Western Church*, p. 191.
15. Nicols, *Corporate Worship*, p. 30.

medied. Most of our modern services make a separation between the Scripture and preached Word by either singing a hymn or hearing an anthem. This is not a pattern that the Reformers subscribed to.

The great emphasis of Reformed ministers of Calvin's day was to preach or exegete the Scriptures so that they could be clearly understood. This would make possible the appropriating of Christ by faith. The purpose of preaching was to bring Christ into the contemporary life of the people. The Reformers saw the gathered assemblies for public worship of much greater importance than private devotional exercises. They placed an importance on the preaching that might shock some of us today, for they felt that preaching and Scripture were of equal revelatory value. Perhaps the reason we are so prone to reject this emphasis on preaching is that so many Protestant sermons are devoid of that serious kind of exposition which was characteristic of Reformation days. The main thing that concerned the Reformers in their preaching was to convey to the "elect" the reality of sins forgiven and thus deliver them from any doubts they might have with respect to their salvation. Sermons were vehicles through which Christ himself was imparted and were given a sacramental quality that we tend to minimize today.

Because of this strong conviction that the Word of God was supreme, Calvin did not hesitate to go all the way in his understanding of the New Testament pattern of worship as it relates to the eucharist. He saw the Lord's Supper as a sacrament in which Christ offered himself to us for the establishment of our souls in him. It was therefore an integral part of Christian worship. The Reformation uncovered the biblical understanding of this sacrament in opposition to the Roman view of transubstantiation. The Reformers utterly rejected the Lord's Supper as a propitiatory sacrifice, along with the false idea that the priest was one who consecrates the sacrifice on behalf of the living and the dead. They believed that the gospel was God's free gift of grace and love from Christ to sinners. It brought to them a reality of God's presence, which they could not merit or earn. For this reason "the gospel was no more compatible with priestly appeasements in masses than with indulgences."[16]

In the observance of the sacrament, the Reformers were not bound to only one particular way of administration. After the sermon and prayer of consecration, or eucharistic prayer, communicants were invited to commune with their Lord. They did so in a variety of ways. Some congregations came forward to the communion table in a long line, receiving the bread at one corner of the chancel and the wine at the other. In the Scottish and Dutch Reformed churches, believers were served at long tables that were set up in the center of the church building or meeting place. The followers of Zwingli and the Anglican reformers served people sitting in their pews. We can see from these practices that most Protestant churches today have changed the form that was originally used by their historic denomination. During the observance of Holy Communion there was joyous but solemn offering of praise. "During the actual distribution of the elements in the Strasburg congregation, they sang one of the triumphant songs from the Psalter . . . , after kneeling the congregation sang the Song of Simeon and rose from their knees."[17]

With this kind of significance attached to the Lord's Supper, "Calvin wanted to observe it at least once a week."[18] Unfortunately, he was voted down by the elders of Geneva, but he took care to express his displeasure with their ruling and hoped that in the future, when times were more settled, the church would amend its decision. Calvin believed that there was "nothing more useful in the Church than the Lord's Supper."[19]

Two of the most important aspects of Reformed worship were the hymns and prayers. In fact, these were seen as one, because hymns were a sung form of prayer. The Reformers in the Presbyterian tradition confined their singing almost entirely to

---

16. Ibid., p. 24.
17. Ibid., p. 51.
18. Thompson, *Liturgies of the Western Church*, p. 185.
19. Calvin, *The Institutes*, Book 4, 14, 7ff.

the Psalter and did not, as did the Lutherans and Anabaptists, develop a hymnody for several centuries. The reason for this limitation of singing to the Psalter was based upon the conviction that one can scarcely improve upon the Psalter and in using it, one was praising God, so to speak, in His own language.[20] They also interpreted the Psalms from a particular point of view. The Reformers used the Psalms so predominantly in their services because they interpreted them Christologically. They felt that the Psalms should be sung because the Church was the New Israel, the people of God. Just as ancient Israel expressed its worship to God through Psalms, the Reformed Church linked itself to that Church by the use of these songs.[21]

Calvin, unlike Zwingli, saw music as the "first gift of God to the Church."[22] He considered music a great force with vigor to move and inflame the hearts of men to invoke and praise God with a more vehement and ardent zeal.[23] Psalm singing was seen as important to "engage the passive people . . ., thus filling worship with a note of adoration,"[24] which Calvin called the "first point of religion."[25] Although Calvin was a man of high culture, he resisted all attempts made by musicians to make the sung liturgy "more aesthetically interesting."[26] While the singing of Psalms was used predominantly, "Reformed churches did incorporate into their worship services the Lord's Prayer and the Apostles' Creed, which were sung, along with other New Testament hymns and Canticles, such as the Magnificat, De Teum, Benedictus, and Nunc Dimittis."[27]

In congregational prayer, Calvin did not permit much latitude. He used prayers "which he felt set forth the basic

---

20. Nicols, *Corporate Worship*, p. 36.

21. Ibid., p. 37.

22. Ibid., p. 34.

23. Ibid., p. 35.

24. Ibid.

25. Thompson, *Liturgies of the Western Church*, p. 189.

26. Nicols, *Corporate Worship*, p. 36.

27. Ibid., p. 40.

doctrines of the Bible and therefore [were] basic to the Christian faith."[28] The Christian life in all its expression was meant to serve the glory of God, who is infinite in greatness, incomparable in essence, boundless in might, and everlasting in immortality. Prayer was a vehicle through which the truths of the Christian faith could be brought before the people in another form other than preaching. While the laity did not participate in the offering of prayer, there was no doubt that as they heard the form of the prayers, the manner in which they were prayed, and the truths they contained, their personal prayer life was molded.

Following the Holy Communion service, Calvin saw the importance of presenting offerings or alms for the service of the Church. This was done without any ceremony, such as we see today in many churches, where the offering plate is elevated or prayers offered for the monies received. Nevertheless, almsgiving was seen as an integral response to the grace of God, and all Christians were expected to tithe their income.

The chief purpose of worship in Calvin's understanding was to glorify God in a public or open way. This is a perfectly legitimate desire and one which should occupy the concern of every Christian desirous of worshiping God in spirit and in truth. But as we examine Calvin's desire to limit the worship services to those spiritual acts which he deemed essential, obliterating certain aspects of worship that had been part of the historical practice by the Church, we have to conclude that sometimes his attitudes were extreme. It has taken Christians in the Reformed tradition many centuries to free themselves from the austerity and inhibiting formality that has become characteristic of these churches. The pattern of Reformed church worship would have been enriched if Calvin had taken the New Testament tradition more seriously, realizing that apostolic Christians were much more flexible, joyous, and unstructured in their worship. Evelyn Underhill expresses my own feelings with respect to Calvin's influence upon Reformed

---

28. Thompson, *Liturgies of the Western Church*, p. 193.

church worship. "In the type of worship which he established we seem to see the result of a great religious experience—the impact of the divine transcendence on the awe-struck soul—and the effort towards a response which is conditioned by a deep sense of creaturely limitation. Calvin desired, as so many real religious souls have done, a completely 'spiritual cultus' ascending toward a completely spiritual Reality, and rejecting all the humble ritual methods and all the sensible signs by which men are led to express their adoration of the Unseen."[29]

## The Church Reformed and Reforming

The great affirmation of the supremacy of Scripture was the foundation upon which the Reformed church's understanding of reformed worship was based. This must ever remain the basis for all Christians, and the expression of that worship in daily living. However, the Reformers, although they were not bound to the Scripture in a legalistic way, manifested a certain inconsistency in their application of Scripture to worship. Calvin insisted that Scripture be regarded as "the holy law and Word of God which is confirmed in the believer's heart by the Holy Spirit and which commands obedience."[30] One cannot help wondering why he ignored some of the biblical patterns that were taken more seriously by the Anabaptists.

Throughout the succeeding centuries, the Reformed church has sought to pattern its worship and church life after Calvin's approach, and in the Scottish tradition of John Knox. For many years a diligent effort was made to follow his teachings. In the nineteenth century, the liberal approach to Scripture and to church doctrine produced a deviation that cut deeply into the life and practice of the Reformed churches. Although there was a preservation of the cardinal doctrines of the faith by retaining

---

29. Evelyn Underhill, *Worship* (New York: Harper and Row, 1936), p. 287.
30. Thompson, *Liturgies of the Western Church*, p. 194.

the great creeds of the Church, there was, nevertheless, a serious departure from the essence of Reformation teaching as it was expressed in local congregations. This brought about a change in the worship patterns of many churches, which included the introduction of musical instruments (the piano and organ); the use of hymns; and shortened sermons, which often were nothing more than moralistic homilies without much scriptural substance. Those Reformed churches which attempted to preserve a more orthodox position led the fight against the liberal influence and were sometimes threatened with inundation. In their reaction to liberalism they tended to conserve the traditional patterns without giving as much concern to the teaching of Scripture as might have occupied their attention.

Reformed church worship has changed considerably since the days of the Reformers, and rightly so. If one believes in the continuing work of the Holy Spirit, then there must be a constant reexamination of our worship in the light of what the Spirit is saying to the Church in its contemporary situation. This is not to imply that the contemporary situation is more authoritative than the Bible or that the worship of the Church must be restyled in order to make it more palatable to the worshiper. The truth of the great themes of Christian faith are basic to the life of the Church today because the Scripture bears faithful witness to what God has done. But there must be a fresh expression of those truths so that the Spirit can still speak to the human heart today. This is why it is necessary for the Reformed church to think of itself as "reformed and reforming." The Reformation was used by God to restore the Gospel to its rightful place. It also attempted to pattern worship of God after its own understanding of the Scriptures and postapostolic practice.

But it did not have the fullness of truth, though it acknowledged the authority of the Bible in all things. It did not have as strong an emphasis as it should have had on such things as the priesthood of all believers, the restoration of the Lord's Supper to weekly observance, or the place of the gifts of the Holy Spirit as they are expressed through the Body of Christ. For this reason, we must insist that the Reformed church of the sixteenth century saw, as we all see, "through a glass darkly."

This also means that in our contemporary situation Reformed Christians must still continue to examine the Scriptures and so bring into the orb of reformed worship all those aspects of New Testament practice which will help to produce a service that is more complete and yet open-ended.

The Reformed church should feel free to incorporate into the worship of the church not only the traditional patterns, which are scripturally based, but also an understanding of what God has been doing in other denominational communions. If, as Paul says, "all things are yours" (1 Cor. 3:21), then there must not be a narrow attitude toward those who have something to say about their experience of the Holy Spirit's activity among them, especially in the area of worship.

Along with the contribution that other churches have made in this area, the Reformed church should recognize the sovereignty of God's Spirit (ruach) as he blows creatively to produce new forms, which would include other aspects of human activity. Calvin was certainly wise in cautioning against anything that is contrived by mere human impulse, but was he wise in limiting the work of the Spirit in only those aspects of worship which he felt were recommended by Scripture as he understood them? Did he not neglect the biblical witness to drama, litanies, musical instruments, poetry, art? If God is the author of all beauty, as the psalmist states—"Out of Zion, the perfection of beauty, hath God shined" (Ps. 50:2)—surely there should be a place for these contributions controlled by the Spirit and the gospel. We can be grateful for those who have led the way in the incorporation of these expressions of worship in our contemporary church life. We must again stress that new forms are for the glorification of God and not for the entertainment of men. But God by his Spirit has been leading the Reformed church along into an enrichment of its services through the utilization of art forms that were not used by the church of the sixteenth century. Although Evelyn Underhill speaks of Reformed churches as being "bleak and stripped," so that real Calvinistic churches are "sacramental, witnessing to the inadequacy of the human over against the divine,"[31] we

---

31. Underhill, *Worship*, p. 286 ff.

recognize that many new Reformed church buildings have expressed the creativity of man in an architecture that is not only beautiful but exciting. The twentieth-century Reformed Christian must recognize that the Spirit is still active and is able to incorporate anything that is legitimate into the sacred worship of God, seeing that "the earth is the Lord's and the fullness thereof" (Ps. 24:1). This will help to deliver worship from static sterility, encouraging Christians to become more creative in their attitude toward worship. We must witness to the living God, who cannot be boxed in by the sixteenth century or tied down to one particular place or form but is as free and active as the wind, blowing where he wants to and leading Christians into a deeper awareness of who he is and how we can worship him.

## Contemporary Worship and Reformation Principles

The United Presbyterian Church of the United States has recognized the importance of giving serious study to the nature of worship and has prepared an excellent statement in its *Book of Worship* (1975). As we reflect on this study, we discern that there has been a sincere attempt to preserve basic Reformation principles and yet to acknowledge the continual leadership of the Holy Spirit as he seeks to inspire us in the worship of God today. The *Book of Worship* recognizes that the Church is a community of faith, "sustained by the power of the Holy Spirit" (16-01-04).[32] It is not a human organization devoting its energies to the maintenance of religious activities. As men acknowledge their sin and are called into the grace of God in Jesus Christ, they are called "to honour God and to offer their lives in thankful devotion to His service" (16-02). Every Christian is called to be a minister to God and to "serve Him through His Church, both in the building of its inner life, and

---

32. Numbers in parentheses refer to page and paragraph citations from the *Book of Worship* (Philadelphia: The Westminster Press, 1972).

to the extension of its service to the world" (16–04). This acknowledgment of the priesthood of all believers, a doctrine taught by the Reformers but scarcely implemented, does not rule out the ordination of special persons to the office of elder. These officers are called for the express purpose of "giving direction and leading of public worship, with special responsibility for the proclamation of the Word of God in preaching, and in the administration of the sacraments" (16–04).

The *Book of Worship* attests to the biblical declaration that God is the center of all of life and calls men to worship. For this reason, "worship lies within the initiative of God, as does all His dealings with men" (17–04). This is an important statement because there is such a heavy emphasis today upon "getting something out of worship," as though the main concern of the minister is to design worship in order to please the members. But what we must continue to emphasize is that there is a revelation of God being made in our worship services, in which he "makes Himself known among His people through His love in Jesus Christ, His claim upon their lives, His abiding presence with them, and His concern for all creation" (17–01). Because he has sent Jesus Christ to redeem the world and to reveal himself, worship is by necessity "a corporate response by the Church to God's mighty act of redemption in Jesus Christ" (17–02). The corporate worship of God's people enables them to set forth the Christian gospel in its essence. Thus worship relates itself to an expression of all the fundamental things that Christians hold together in common. In the various aspects of worship, which include Scripture, sermon, and sacraments, "it is Jesus Christ who confronts men in order that they might be moved by the Holy Spirit to respond in adoration of God for His steadfast love" (17–03). The grace of God, which has taken hold of the believer, makes it possible for him to "worship God at any time for all time has been redeemed by Him" (17–04). But from the beginning of the Church's history there has been one day called the Lord's Day, when Christians gather specifically to worship God and to praise him for the Resurrection. Thus, "every public service of worship witnesses to God's continuing power over sin and death" (17–04).

In chapter three of the *Book of Worship*, the Presbyterian

church sets forth the positive creative activity of the Holy Spirit, as he utilizes the Scripture, sermon, and sacrament for the mediating of Christ to the individual heart. The Church as a worshiping community comes together to hear God's Word, because it "is under the authority of Jesus Christ and that Word must be preached, not only to the world, but also to the Church itself" (18–01). This statement links the Church of today with our forefathers in the sixteenth-century Reformation, who placed such high regard upon the Word for the Church itself.

The reading of Scripture proclaims the mighty acts of God in history. The sermon is an exposition of that written word, with the purpose of confronting each person in a contemporary way with the authority of Jesus in their lives. Thus there is a hearing and a speaking action that must be held together in worship. Sacraments, for the sake of order, are administered traditionally by the minister, but this does not mean that he has an intrinsic position of authority. This is certainly one area where the Reformed church today needs to question its understanding of the minister as he relates to the whole body of believers. Is the observance of the sacrament of the Lord's Supper to be bound up with the minister as the only one qualified to administer? While it may be recognized that he acts only on behalf of Christ and His Church, where does the lay person fit into this understanding?

It is an important insight made by the *Book of Worship* that public worship does not need to be bound by prescribed forms, for in so doing there is a robbing of the Christian of that liberty which sets him free from legalistic worship. At the same time, whatever is done in a service of worship must be done with a sense of decency and order (19–01). The task of the pastor as liturgist is to see that the worship of God is engaged in with complete loyalty to those aspects of worship which are set forth in the Scriptures and in the New Testament Church. There is meant to be a sensitivity to the historic experience of the Church throughout the ages. Thus the Church today can appropriate for her use those forms and usages which set forth the gospel most helpfully. Whatever forms are utilized, it is not the form itself that is important but the attitude of the heart toward God. Thus "men worship God when they respond in obedience to His Word, singing forth His praise, praying to Him, and sharing in the sacraments which God has provided" (19–02). The Church is a community of believers and therefore has every right to participate in the fullest measure in the service and not to be indifferent observers to something that is being conducted by the minister and the choir. Again this necessitates a recognition of the importance of the "priesthood of all believers." When this is recognized, "members of the congregation may be asked to assist in the conduct of the worship, thus bearing witness that leadership in public worship is delegated as a principle of order by the Church and is not the exclusive privilege of those set apart by ordination" (19–03). What a great step in the right direction this would have been if the sixteenth-century Reformers had been so perceptive.

The section on prayer is surely one of the most helpful statements made on this subject for the benefit of expressing the priestly involvement of all the members of the church. As we have stated, the doctrine of the priesthood of all believers was not expressed as practically as it could have been by the Reformers. This is why the Church must continue to reform itself in the light of God's Word. Thus the confession contained in this document is asserting the biblical principle when it insists

> at appropriate times in the service all present are to pray together. Certain prayers, particularly those offered by all the people may be drawn from Scripture and the liturgical heritage of Christendom, and made the people's own. The leader may bid the people to pray in litanies, responses, and in silent prayer. It is also fitting that special prayers be offered relating to specific and urgent needs of individual persons, the congregation and the world. And the conclusion of such prayers, as are spoken by the leader of worship, the people's response in the spoken "amen" as an affirmation that such prayers are their own, to which they give common consent [19–03].

The *Book of Worship* recognizes the prominent place that sung praise of God has in the context of Christian worship. "The true choir for the singing of praise is the entire congregation" (19–03). Special auxiliary choirs may be drawn up from the membership of the congregation and when it sings it is "representing the congregation." How important is this injunction for the Presbyterian church today, because there is an observable overemphasis upon choir music, which needs to be brought into balance. One rejoices in the instruction in the *Book of Forms* that music presented by the choir must be consistent with the beliefs of the Church and not the personal whims of the choirmaster or organist and that music also should be a medium through which praise from the congregation is offered while listening. Thus the music should be "common music" and not highly technical scores that might be presented at a concert by a professionally trained choir. The choir provides certain individuals in the church with musical gifts an opportunity to offer to God the gratitude they have for those gifts which he has bestowed. Above all, the hymns and choir selections must be centered on the great themes of Christian faith, and not hymns of witness. The presentation of choral praise must also give attention to meaningfulness, which indicates that words should be clear, understood, and contemporary. A revolution in most church choirs would take place if this injunction were taken seriously.

The Reformed church tended to downplay the liturgical year, and this has been one of the weaknesses of our church historically. However, we can be grateful that in recent years there has been the reinstitution of the great festivals of the church year, which help to center the thoughts of Christians upon the mighty acts of God. The *Book of Forms* recognizes this and indicates that though the chief purpose of a service is the presentation of the Gospel, there are seasons when Christians should stress the unique acts of God in the Incarnation, the death and Resurrection of Christ, the outpouring of the Holy Spirit, and Christ's Ascension. "At all of these services the one objective is to glorify God who is the initiator of all these redemptive events in history. Other days which may be observed must not minimize these cardinal events, and must set forth what Scripture teaches about the theme that is being emphasized" (19–04).

The *Book of Worship* concurs with the Reformers that the worship of God must include the confession of sin, "since God is the God of holy, redeeming love, who in Jesus Christ has condemned sin by conquering its power" (19–05). Confessions of sin should be made by the whole congregation and also by individual private confessions. Then they should be followed by a "declaration of the assurance of forgiveness in Christ" (19–05).

Like the Reformers, the *Book of Worship* sees the sermon as an integral part of worship, "since Scripture is the record of God's mighty acts in making Himself known to men, and also a means by which through the power of the Holy Spirit, God makes Himself known to men today" (19–06). "Before the preaching of the Word, prayer should be offered for the divine illumination of the Word, so that all may understand and respond. The leader of the service may call upon God to so anoint him as He did men of old, that the words of men may become the Word of God" (19–06). Certainly this prayer should be one of the most important in the service and not just a little collect, which has a tendency to become trite and regarded as unimportant.

The sermon, of course, is meant to be expounded with deep concern that the congregation hear what God has said and not what men might think. The preacher as the instrument through which this part of the service takes place must be recognized by the people as worthy of his teaching office. It is heartening that the *Book of Forms* continues to stress a principle that the Reformers emphasized, that "through the Word of God incarnate in Jesus Christ, the sermon is a witness to what God has done through Him, it must be heard in faith and received as the living Word of God" (19–06). Scripture should be taught through lessons, but this does not mean that the sermon cannot be expressed in anything other than the traditional form. The *Book of Worship* is alert to the possibility of various ways to present God's truth. Such innovations include singing a hymn after each point is made; making a partial presentation and then asking the people to interact, then bringing that word to a conclusion by a clarification or enlargement of what has been said by the leader. These innovations serve to enrich the sermonic presentation and keep the people alive to the hearing of God's Word.

It is gratifying to have the *Book of Worship* stress the significance of the Lord's Supper, although it still seeks to preserve a custom of Presbyterian history—the quarterly communion. But it insists that Holy Communion can be held on any occasion. It is meant to be fittingly observed, which is interpreted as "following the proclamation of the Word." This is debatable. The Word of God can come home to the heart through the singing of hymns just as much as in the presentation of a sermon, and thus it is as possible to enter joyously into the celebration of Holy Communion after sung praise has been offered as it is to engage in this sacrament following the spoken sermon. Music has a power to lift the spirit to God with such emotion that to follow the Holy Communion service often seems more appropriate than waiting until an exposition of Scripture has been given.

The Reformed church today is seeking to continue its obligation to itself and to the world by studying the necessary ingredients of worship and by seeking to help people understand what they are doing when they engage in public worship. This is one of the adventures of faith that happily engages people in the Westminster Fellowship. Everyone is encouraged to make his contribution to the worship of God, and so there is an emphasis on silence and the gifts of the Spirit. These are two aspects of worship stressed by the Quakers and the Pentecostals and which have had very little place in the worship of the Reformed churches. Here is an area where we need to give ourselves to deeper study and openness to what the Spirit wants to say to us today.

# Chapter 2

Calvin, John. *The Institutes of the Christian Religion,* (Book 4). Philadelphia: The Westminster Press, 1959.

Green, Michael. *I Believe in the Holy Spirit.* Grand Rapids: William B. Eerdman's, 1975.

Nicols, James Hastings. *Corporate Worship in the Reformed Tradition.* Philadelphia: The Westminster Press, 1968.

Thompson, Bard. *Liturgies of the Western Church.* New York: New American Library, 1961.

Underhill, Evelyn. *Worship.* New York: Harper and Row, 1936.

# Chapter 3.  The Priesthood of All Believers and Pastoral Leadership in Worship

IF WORSHIP IS TO BE patterned upon the example of the New Testament and the traditions of the early Church, which are consistent with Scripture, then the pastor must give himself to a diligent understanding of the nature of the Church and his role in it. This will undoubtedly lead to a reaffirmation of the Reformed church doctrine of the "priesthood of all believers." What does this concept of the Church mean in terms of worship, and its relationship to the pastor who is called to give leadership to the congregation? These are pertinent questions which must be faced squarely.

The doctrine of the priesthood of all believers is an integral part of the Reformed church teaching, yet it is a greatly neglected area. It is the subordination of this doctrine that has created the sharp division between the clergy and the laity, a division which the sixteenth-century Reformers did not wish to make. It nevertheless has happened and has strongly affected the Reformed churches as they developed historically. Most Christians in the Church see themselves as "only laymen" and feel that they have very little to contribute in the service, apart from a sincere heart, worshiping God through silent prayer, congregation singing, giving of offerings, and participating in the Lord's Supper. But all these aspects of worship must be seen as subordinate to the preacher's role in expounding the Word of God. These privileges granted him in worship date back to the Reformation and have been the characteristic involvement of

Reformed church Christians in their worship services. But is this an adequate understanding of the New Testament and the concept of pastor and people? Did the Reformation give back to the people their rightful place in the church worship participation?

This question necessitates a brief survey of what the Reformers said about this all-important doctrine of priesthood of all believers, especially as it relates to public worship. It is generally concluded that the Reformers, especially Luther and Calvin, were men of deep biblical commitment. They wanted the Church to be restored to the pattern of Scripture and early Church tradition. We know that they differed somewhat in the emphasis they placed upon scriptural injunctions. Luther did not want to rid the Church of anything that was not inconsistent with scriptural teaching, but Calvin went a step further and claimed that God wanted only that spiritual worship which was clearly stipulated in his Word. Both were men rooted in the Scriptures as far as their desire for the revelation of the glory of God in the worship services.

One of the doctrines that had to be faced at this time was that of the priesthood. What did the Bible say about priesthood and its place in the Church? The medieval church was "priest ridden" in the opinion of the Reformers, and this accusation is confirmed by many contemporary scholars of the Roman Catholic church. It is generally recognized that the priesthood of the Roman Catholic church was a development from the simplicity of the New Testament understanding to the highly regulated hierarchy of the medieval and modern Roman Catholic church. We can be grateful that there are some Catholic scholars who are attempting to remodel their church's understanding of the priesthood after biblical patterns, but they are having difficulty doing it because of the attitude of the papacy. But many statements are being made by these scholars concerning the nature of the Church and the priesthood that the Reformers would have welcomed in their day. Realizing that the Church is a "royal priesthood" (1 Peter 2:5,9), some Catholic writers have made some radical statements concerning the priesthood and the laity.

John M. Todd, a Paulist priest, writes that the laity are those who are called to "truly share in all three offices of priest, prophet, and king."[1] He asserts that "by our baptism and confirmation we share in the priesthood of Christ."[2] "We are all of us the priests of brotherly love, fatherly love, family love. We are the priests of unity. Those ordained to the ministerial priesthood have a special task, but all Christians share in the common priesthood."[3] Another priest recognizes the Catholic church's need to grapple more intensely with its concept of the priesthood when he writes, "Priests themselves find it difficult to determine exactly where they belong in the people of God. They even ask what is the use of their being priests."[4]

He feels that the problem of the nature of the priesthood was raised by Vatican 2 and unanswered, though the council declared that "all baptized share in the priesthood of Christ."[5] It is recognized by Msgr. Gerard Philips that Catholics are not accustomed to hearing that "the laity is the Church."[6]

It seems from recent Catholic studies that there is a tension between their understanding of the laity as priests unto God and the special priesthood that has been the particular role of the Catholic church to defend. On one hand one hears that the laity are called to function as priests; but on the other hand there are voices that express the feelings of a conservative, such as Pope Pius XII: "Consequently the laity must have an ever clearer consciousness, not only of belonging to the Church, but being the Church, that is the community of the faithful on earth [and then he adds the peculiar Catholic understanding of priesthood] under the guidance of their common leader the Pope and the bishops in communion with him."[7] Some

---

1. John M. Todd, *The Laity: The People of God* (New York: Paulist Press, 1958, p. 15.

2. Ibid.

3. Ibid.

4. Andre Feuillet, *The Priesthood of Christ and His Ministers* (Garden City, New York: Doubleday & Co., 1975), p. 13.

5. Ibid.

6. Msgr. Gerard Philips, *The Priesthood of Believers: The Role of the Laity in the Church* (Notre Dame: Pides Publishers, 1972), p. 5.

7. Ibid.

Catholic writers are honest enough to see what the Reformers grasped so clearly, that "the letter of the Hebrews asserts very emphatically there is only one Priest, Christ, and only one sacrifice, that one offered by Christ on Golgotha. The letter to the Hebrews gives no hint that in addition to the Incarnate Son of God, ordinary men could not be considered as priests in the Christian dispensation."[8] But having said this, Feuillet reverts to the persistent Catholic claim when he writes, "I have shown that Jesus was truly a priest and that he intended to bestow authority upon his apostles and their successors quite distinct from the priesthood common to all baptized."[9]

It is unfortunate that Catholic writers and theologians today are not as consistent in their teaching about the priesthood of all believers as were the Reformers of the sixteenth century. Calvin and Luther were absolutely clear that in Christ's priesthood all special priesthoods were abolished and that through his merits all believers share in his priesthood. Luther was most forceful when he declared that "all believers share a common dignity. It cannot be said that some Christians belong to a religious class and others do not."[10] Cyril Eastwood quotes Luther directly, "For all Christians whatsoever really and truly belong to the religious class and there is no difference among them except in so far as they do different work . . ., for baptism, Gospel and faith alone make men religious and create a Christian people."[11] In his Reformation writings, Luther protested "that Christ did not give the keys to Peter and his successors personally, but to the whole Church and congregation."[12]

This understanding of the priesthood of all believers must be discerned carefully because there are some modern Protestants who see it as a teaching that supports private interpretation of Scripture. But the Reformers did not develop this doctrine in

---

8. Feuillet, *Priesthood of Christ and His Ministers*, p. 12.

9. Ibid., p. 239.

10. Cyril Eastwood, *The Priesthood of All Believers* (London: Epworth Press, 1960), p. 12.

11. Ibid., p. 12.

12. Ibid., p. 34.

that direction; they were simply asserting that all believers are called to share in a priestly ministry before God and are not to be controlled by one particular group of men called "priests." Reformation teaching did not throw out the biblical office of pastor–teacher (Eph. 4:14) but simply grasped its significance in a truly apostolic way. "Luther's view is that the Word is not received through ordination but through a call to service, and if ordination does take place, it is not integral to the ministry. Anyone who receives a call holds the ministry independent of ordination. It follows that ordination is only a public confirmation of a call, and what is received in calling is not a special gift or grace or power, but a commission."[13] Pastors still have an important role in the Church, but it is a divine call that makes a man a pastor, not some ordination rite. All true Christians are called to be ministers (Eph. 4:14–16), and that is why Luther is careful to emphasize that "all Christians being priests possess equal authority and that no one may exercise it without the confirmation of the congregation of the faithful."[14]

In the writings of Calvin we hear the same emphasis. He was convinced that on the basis of divine election every Christian is called to serve God in a priestly way. J.M. Barkley (quoted by Eastwood) underscores Calvin's attitude toward laymen when he writes, "all men are priests in their daily vocations. All are priests though their duties vary according to their calling. The only real farmer is a Christian farmer, the only true doctor is a Christian doctor, the only real mother is a Christian mother, the only real man is a Christian man, and so on, covering every detail and aspect and station in life."[15]

Because Calvin saw this as the basic foundation of the priesthood of all believers, he contended that the Roman hierarchy had taken upon itself privileges that belonged to the whole Church. At the same time, the priesthood of all believers does not eliminate the order of pastor. He saw the difference

---

13. Ibid., p. 40.
14. Ibid., p. 41.
15. Ibid., p. 73. Quoted from J.M. Barkley, *Presbyterianism*, p. 18.

between the priesthood and the ministry which is intrinsic to the Pauline understanding of the Church and the laity. Quoting from P. Schaff's book, *The Creeds of the Evangelical Protestant Churches*, Eastwood draws our attention to the Second Helvetic Confession. "Accordingly there are great differences between a priesthood and a ministry. For the former is common to all Christians, as we have just said, but the same is not so with the latter. We have not removed the ministry out of the midst of the Church when we have cast the papalistic priesthood out of the Church of Christ."[16] Sixteenth-century Protestantism was clearly concerned to eliminate sacradotalism on the basis of the New Testament teaching that Christ, and Christ alone, is the One High Priest with an unchangeable priesthood (Heb. 7:24). Christ is the only Mediator (a word he preferred to priest) between God and man. There is no priesthood apart from him, "for we who are polluted in ourselves have been made priests in and through Him."[17]

The sad factor in all of this biblical teaching by the two greatest Reformers of the Reformation is that it was not integrated into the life of the Church as it might have been. We should not condemn the Reformers at this point, for tremendous strides were taken to reform the church at a very difficult time. Other things engrossed their attention, and the training of adequate pastors for the church was one of them. But this concern for suitable pastor–teachers to lead the people led to an overemphasis upon pastoral leadership. It has taken several centuries of increasing deterioration of church life for us to become aware of the necessity to restore the laity to the place God intended them to have.

As we rejoice in the degree of Reformation which the sixteenth century Reformers brought about, we cannot ignore that there were some serious failures that have prevailed until today. The Reformers, as we know, were men of their times and

---

16. Ibid., p. 78.

17. Kerr, Hugh Thomson, *A Compend of the Institutes of the Christian Religion* (Philadelphia: Presbyterian Board of Education, 1939), p. 80.

inherited the individualism and clericalism of the medieval church. "This spirit of clericalism survived in the Reformed Church, reflected in the dominant role of the minister as he conducted the services of public worship."[18] Worship has remained largely what it was before the Reformation, a service conducted almost entirely by the minister. We must agree with Stephen Winnard when he writes, "To this day, especially in Reformed and Free Church traditions, church worship is dominated by the man in the pulpit to whom most of the service has been handed over. Apart from the singing, the congregation is reduced to the role of listening for at least three quarters of the service."[19]

The priesthood of all believers has not been recovered in most Protestant churches because of this "error of verbalism."[20] This kind of verbalism has overemphasized the pastor's role and reduced the significance of the laity to such a degree that most lay people feel inferior to the minister in the area of expression and thus have become more and more passive, to the point of saying nothing.

Charismatic congregations in the Reformed tradition have begun to experience an awakening that centers in a rediscovery of the manifestations of the gifts of the Holy Spirit. If these gifts are to be expressed, as 1 Corinthians 12 and 14 clearly indicate, then each lay person will need to accept himself more radically as a priest of God. This compels the membership of the church to regard themselves as "kings and priests unto God" in a manner that has not been characteristic of most Protestant churches.

The concept of the priesthood was one that the early Christians inherited from their association with Judaism. The Old Testament knew a priestly class that offered sacrifices, but this sacrificial system passed away because of the perfect atoning work of Christ on the cross. His sacrifice eliminated any human intermediary to intercede on the people's behalf. Christ's heavenly ministry was sufficient. The early Christians not only

---

18. Stephen Winnard, *The Reformation of Our Worship* (Richmond: John Knox Press, 1964), p. 105.

19. Ibid.

20. Ibid.

saw Christ as their priest, but they also saw themselves as a new priesthood (1 Pet. 2:5,9; Rev. 1:55ff).

Four great principles emerged in the early Church because of this Christological understanding of priesthood. God everywhere takes the initiative in appointing priests. (b) It is He who makes us kings and priests, just as priests were appointed by God in the Old Testament to represent sinners before God, so every Christian has this responsibility. (c) Because Christ has made the perfect sacrifice, Christians are called to lay down their lives for their brethren as part of their priestly calling. (d) Because Christ is our Great Interceder, Christians are initiated into a ministry of intercession which is similar to Christ's priestly ministry of intercession in Romans 8.[21]

When we begin to apply these truths concerning the priesthood of believers, particularly as they relate to the act of public worship, we see that it means much more than it did in the past. Each worshiper has a right to approach God directly, without the intervention of any priestly medium. If Christians are priests, then "they have every right to act as priests on behalf of his fellow believers."[22] When we grasp the nature of our relationship to one another in the Body of Christ, "then it assigns the action of worship to all the congregation and thus it raises and answers the problems when we speak of congregation participation."[23] Reformed churches experiencing renewal charismatically must realize "that for us, as for the primitive Christian community, we need no priests because the congregation consists of nothing but priests and our Protestant task is not so much the abolition of priesthood, as we are wont to say, but the abolition of the laity."[24] This fresh discovery does not mean that we should eliminate the function of the pastor as a leader in worship, but theologically it does mean that "the pastor is no more priest than people, and both participate in what the other does."[25]

21. Everett F. Harrison, ed., *Baker's Dictionary of the Bible*, 4th ed., (Grand Rapids: Baker House, 1969), pp. 419–20.

22. Paul Hoon, *The Integrity of Worship* (Nashville: Abingdon Press, 1975), p. 105.

23. Ibid.

24. Ibid.

25. Ibid.

What did this mean for a congregation like the Westminster Fellowship, which was experiencing charismatic renewal? First of all, individual Christians began to have a sense of importance as to who they were in Christ. Because their participation was welcomed in the service at every appropriate point, those who took seriously their calling in Christ no longer spoke of themselves as "mere laymen." They felt honored to be called priests unto God, and they knew that they were doing something significant when they embarked (hesitantly at first) upon participation in the worship of God in a manner not encouraged before.

As they gathered for worship, they began to realize in a new and emancipating way that every Christian has his or her role to play in worship. From studying 1 Corinthians and other Scriptures, they were uncertain whether every member should take part in the services, but certainly they must be set free to do so, particularly the men. Conscious of their involvement in charismatic renewal, they were sensitive to the fact that the Corinthian church had permitted its services to become chaotic and needed some definite guidelines on the nature of worship, which is led by the Spirit. As the members of the congregation felt free to announce a hymn they felt suitable, or to join in prayers of thanksgiving and intercession, to take part in the reading of Scripture when invited, to pass the elements of Communion from one to another with a word of blessing or encouragement, to give the peace of God to each other, to lay hands on those needing and requesting prayer, to respond to the sermon when it was preached, and to share with one another in small groups what the sermon had said to them, they discovered that they were in the tradition of the apostles and second-century Christians and that "worship is corporate, communal and congregational."[26]

They also discovered by experience that Spirit-led worship, like every other form of worship, has its negative and positive possibilities. On the positive side, when everyone is encouraged to engage in worship, it gives full expression to the validity of the Church as the living Body of Christ. But when charismatic

---

26. Winnard, *The Reformation of Our Worship*, p. 96.

worship is lacking control, it can degenerate, as classical Pentecostal worship has often shown, into "blatant egoism, emotionalism, individualism, the desire to show off, rivalry, overevaluation of the spectacular, disorder."[27] Charismatics must be committed to the scriptural principle that all things should be done decently and in order (1 Cor. 14:40). There must be the prayerful desire that God will keep worshipers from any excess, thus quenching the Spirit from operating in the lives of people as they feel moved by the Lord, or from creating disorder by not controlling more overt members who need to be subject to the Body as well as to the Lord.

The study of Church history enables us to see that throughout the long history of its existence, Christians have attempted to keep the free spontaneous element in worship prevalent. From our study of the Montanists of the third century, the Quakers of the sixteenth and seventeenth centuries, and the Plymouth Brethren and Pentecostals of the nineteenth and twentieth centuries, we find that this attempt to preserve the unpredictable dimension in worship has been expressed. There is a need for faithfulness to the Reformed church heritage, with its strong emphasis upon the Word of God and the sacraments, especially the restoration of the Lord's Supper to a weekly observance, as Calvin had pleaded for in Geneva, with disappointing results. But there is greater need for congregations of priestly men and women who permit the Holy Spirit to guide and direct in the worship as it pleases him. If this begins to happen, the pastor and the people will discover that they have overcome the "usurption by the ordained ministry of those functions which should be engaged in by the laity. The clergy and laity are not in competition with one another, but are as one body offering praise to the Lord, each performing its own ministry."[28]

If this present weakness in the worship of most Protestant churches is to be overcome, each member in the Body must be encouraged to come to the services prepared to take part in the fullest possible measure. This may take place over a period of

---

27. Ibid., p. 101.
28. Ibid., p. 96.

time. Eventually, it will result in the deliverance of worship from the boredom that so often characterizes the services of the Reformed churches. Instead of the traditional Church service hour of eleven to twelve, many charismatic churches worshiping in the Reformed tradition have found themselves worshiping from ten to twelve-thirty with such joy and blessing that they hardly can break away from one another. They have proven that the more the laity are encouraged to participate in worship governed by Jesus' injunction "in spirit and in truth," the more they not only rejoice in their priesthood but also have a stronger sense of their historic continuity with the apostolic Church of New Testament times.

---

## Chapter 3

Eastwood, Cyril. *The Priesthood of All Believers*. London: Epworth Press, 1960.

Feuillet, Andre. *The Priesthood of Christ and His Ministers*. Garden City, New York: Doubleday & Co., 1975.

Graham, W. Fred. *John Calvin, The Constructive Revolutionary*. Richmond: John Knox Press, 1970.

Harrison, Everett F., ed. *Baker's Dictionary of Theology*. 4th ed. Grand Rapids: Baker House, 1969.

Hoon, Paul. *The Integrity of Worship*. Nashville: Abingdon Press, 1971.

Kerr, Hugh Thomson, ed. *A Compend of the Institutes of the Christian Religion*. Philadelphia: Presbyterian Board of Christian Education, 1939.

Luther, Martin. *Luther's Works*. Philadelphia: Fortress Press, 1970.

Philips, Msgr. Gerard. *The Priesthood of Believers: The Role of the Laity in the Church*. Notre Dame: Pides Publishers, 1972.

Rahner, Karl. *The Priesthood*. New York: The Seabury Press, 1973.

Todd, John M. *The Laity: The People of God*. New York: Paulist Press, 1958.

Winnard, Stephen. *The Reformation of Our Worship*. Richmond: John Knox Press, 1964.

# Chapter 4. Practical Ways of Involving the Laity in Worship

## (A) The Reading and Preaching of the Word

THE BARRIERS BETWEEN pastor and people will become less and less significant as a deepening sense of equality before God develops. Those who put the pastor on a high pedestal must realize that it is wrong for him and for them. Indeed, the pendulum can swing in two directions. He may be given a place that makes him superior to other members of the congregation, or it may be that a congregation chooses to have no pastor at all. The early Church seemed to have had a plurality of pastors, and this is the pattern of a number of evangelical churches today, particularly the Plymouth Brethren. This challenges members of the Reformed churches to do some investigation into the nature of the ministry.

Paul's letter to the Ephesians is particularly helpful in directing the way we may have to take with respect to a special pastoral ministry, as well as in gaining a fresh appreciation of the nature of the laity. In his great Pauline letter, he states that God has set some in the Church in special offices, and these persons are gifts (doria) to the Church. There were first apostles, then prophets, then evangelists, followed by pastor–teachers. The purpose of their unique ministry is to equip the "saints for the work of the ministry" (Eph. 4:11–12). This seems to indicate that there is a place for the specially called, trained, ordained, pastor; whose primary task is to preach God's Word. This is meant to build up the people of God in faith and commitment, so that they may do the work of the ministry, i.e., evangelism, visitation of the poor and sick, and social action. The total congregation is called to minister, and it is probably an error to describe the pastor–teacher as a "minister." This tends to separate the pastor from his people and to give the impression that their roles as ministers are secondary to his.

Reformed congregations need to enter into a fresh awareness of the Spirit's power and ministry in the life of the Church. But in this discovery they must not turn away from the Reformed understanding of the pastor's ministry without first understanding what the Reformers taught. Christians in the Reformed tradition are primarily concerned with the teachings of John Calvin, discovering in his *Institutes of the Christian Religion* that he has given some clear direction on what the pastor is meant to be and to do. Calvin writes that when the Lord sent forth his apostles, he commissioned them to preach the gospel and to baptize all believers for the remission of sins; to behold the sacred, inviolable and perpetual law imposed on those who call themselves the successors to the apostles. He commands them to preach the gospel and to administer the sacraments. Hence he concludes that those who neglect both of these duties have no pretension to the character of the apostles.[1] He makes it very clear that pastors are to depend entirely upon the Lord for their ministry, because it is only the Holy Spirit who can make the Word of God come alive. When pastors are called to their office it was at the same time enjoined that they should bring forth nothing of themselves, but should speak from the mouth of the Lord. Nor did he send them forth in public to address the people before he had instructed them what they should say that they should speak nothing beside his Word.[2]

Rather than eliminate the pastor–teacher role from the Church, there is a need to realize how important it is to underscore the apostolic concept of the pastor's calling, not merely because it is the tradition of the Reformed churches but also

---

1. John Calvin, *The Institutes of the Christian Religion*, (Philadelphia: The Westminster Press, 1959), Book 4, p. 1058.
2. Ibid., Book 4, pp. 1150–1151.

because it is basic to biblical thought. The importance of pastors in Calvin's thought is again emphasized.

> We see that though God could easily make His people perfect in a single moment, yet it was not His will that they should grow to mature age, but under the education of the Church. We see the means expressed — the preaching of the heavenly doctrine assigned to pastors. We see that all are placed under the same regulation in order that they may submit themselves in gentleness and docility of mind to be governed by pastors who are appointed for that purpose.... It is a good proof of our obedience when we listen to His ministers, just as if He were addressing us Himself, and on the other hand, He has provided for our infirmity by choosing to address us through a medium of human interpreters that He may sweetly allure us to Him, rather than drive us away from Him by His thunder.[3]

To reject the oversight and ministry of a specially trained, ordained pastor is contrary to Scripture. But this compels us to think seriously about the role of lay people, especially as it relates to the hearing of the Word of God through a preached sermon. While pastors are important for the preaching of the Word, as John Killenger points out, "with the advent of Luther, Zwingli, Calvin and Knox, preaching began to assume a greater significance than other elements of the Church service,"[4] there must be an examination of this form of communication. Important as preaching is, most congregations have not understood its importance and relevance as they should. We must recognize that "there is no substitute for preaching in worship . . ., it provides the proclamatory thrust without which the Church is never formed and worship is never made possible. It complements the creedal, poetic nature of the liturgy and keeps before the mind the absolute contemporaneity of the gospel. Nowhere else, either in worship, or in the wide, wide world, does God confront us so directly, or mediate Himself so intoxicatingly as He does in the preaching of the Word."[5] The

3. Ibid., Book 4, 1, 5.
4. John Killinger, *The Centrality of Preaching in the Total Task of The Ministry* (Waco, Texas: Word Books, 1969), p. 36.
5. Ibid., p. 51.

sermon is central, but we often fail to recognize its relationship to the other parts of the service. There is a great need to understand what John Killenger states so powerfully: "The sermon conceived and effectually preached is the point of focus which gives true depth and shading and meaning to the rest of the picture, so that nothing in the service, not the sublimest praising or a prayer, or the slightest tremor is lost or undervalued."[6] When we begin to appreciate the importance that the Reformers placed upon the sermon, we will see that it was not just because the great mass of church members in those days were grossly ignorant of Scripture and needed regular teaching; but, rather, that every part of the Christian worship service is strengthened and "exalted to its true status, as the sermon brings the Word from beyond to bear upon them and illumine them, actualizing them and contemporizing them."[7]

With this new appreciation for biblical preaching the pastor will feel more inclined toward expository preaching than ever before, and the people will be more anxious to receive it regularly. But expository preaching has a goal to achieve, which should bind us together in the desire to minister one to another. William Malcomson expresses the concern that preaching be relevant to human needs. "We need to do three things, first, we need to direct our preaching to men and women at the point of their basic needs, two, to shed the light of the gospel on those needs, and three, to challenge the people to accept what Christ offers."[8] As pastors begin to do this kind of preaching, there will be a heartening response on the part of the congregation in terms of the exposure of the circumstances of their lives to the Word of God.

Along with the realization that expository preaching must touch the lives of people, "where they live," it is important to see the whole service ministering to those needs in the context not only of the preached word but also of the hymns, prayers, and

---

6. Ibid., p. 36.

7. Ibid., p. 43.

8. William L. Malcomson, *The Preaching Event* (Philadelphia: The Westminster Press, 1968), p. 17.

other responses, such as communion. It thus becomes impossible to describe these elements of worship as "the preliminaries." The whole service is meant to be a channel by which we become conscious of our responsibility not only to worship the true and living God but also to bring our needs and those of others to him. "Thus, when the congregation gathers, it should be much more than a company of individuals brought together for an hour with no sense of belonging to one another."[9] Corporate worship means that every individual's horizon is enlarged, not only of God but of themselves as members one of another.

*New Forms of Communication.* As we live in the twentieth century, sensitive to the great changes that are taking place around us in the world and in the church, the traditional concept of the sermon as understood from the Reformed point of view has to be examined anew. This is not so much in terms of its place and importance in the service but, rather, in terms of the form it should take. We have to accept the principle that the Church should be reformed and reforming. If it is a reforming community, then "real communication is not static and can seldom be accomplished for long without experimentation and innovation."[10] We know that many people are becoming unhappy with an inflexible, monologue approach to the sermon, which has been so long accepted by Protestantism that we hardly dare challenge its sacrosanct position. We are convinced that "it would be especially wrong in religion not to encourage newness. What is heard too long and seen and felt too long in the same manner, inevitably becomes idolatrous."[11] Change for the sake of change is not our goal but to improve the manner in which the Word of God comes home to our hearts. Many Christians confess that pastors' sermons that are excellent and helpful in church are hardly remembered in any practical way

9. Thomas M. Morrow, *Worship and Preaching* (London: Epworth Press, 1956), p. 17.
10. John Killinger, *Experimental Preaching* (Nashville: Abingdon Press, 1973), p. 9.
11. Ibid., p. 11.

by Wednesday or Thursday. We must realize that in the light of human perception and the dynamics of learning, "there is a need for a constant state of change and disorientation, so that the mind can strive constantly to perceive and reknow the object of devotion otherwise taken for granted."[12]

Of course, changing the format of anything in the Presbyterian and Reformed tradition can be quite traumatic for some people. The Church is often kept from moving forward under the leadership of the Spirit because the "religious mind" is often a closed mind. "It tends to accept uncritically the doctrines and dogmas recommended by leaders unmindful of the grossly human and secular conditions in which the teachings originally took shape. Then it automatically rules out the other possibilities and spends its energies trying to force all new experiences and acquisitions of knowledge into conformity."[13]

This sense of need for change should be based upon two things. First, as we study the New Testament patterns of worship we see that the early Church worship had a dimension that is missing in Reformed Church worship. The early Christians took a much more active part in worship than was typical of the Reformation and the ensuing centuries of Protestantism. There was a dialogue that went on between the people and those leading them in worship. Lay people were not considered passive receivers but active participants as they responded to the Word of God not only in an inward act of faith but also in the outward testimony of God's action in their lives as a result of that Word acting upon them. This concept of the dialogue sermon presentation began to take hold of the Westminster Fellowship, and they wanted to know if it could be achieved. Secondly, there must be a freedom for people to respond to the Word of God by the exercise of whatever gifts the Spirit might call forth in the service.

The Westminster Fellowship became aware of a new form of sermon presentation called the "dialogue" sermon, which captivated their minds with its possibilities. This is a form that

---

12. Ibid.
13. Ibid., p. 14.

was utilized by the apostolic church up to the fourth century. In that sense it was not "new" but was being freshly rediscovered. The early Church had no professional clergy as we understand it today; as a result there was a good deal of informality and spontaneous response.

> The worship in the early Church, like its evangelism, was personal and informal. There was little structure and elaborate liturgy developed slowly. The New Testament reports conversation between the disciples and Jesus and the people they confronted in their attempts to spread the good news. But there is little clear statement in the New Testament of the kind of worship used by the first century Christians. We do have St. Paul's interpretation of worship in 1 Corinthians 14:26-40 which implies that there members of the congregation were free to share orally, as they were moved by the Spirit, their concerns and ideas. Each person in the assembly was free to contribute his own thoughts regarding the interpretation and understanding of God's Word.[14]

"This form was also known and practiced by such men as Chrysostom."[15] We read of Augustine of Hippo, who seemed to be involved with a constant dialogue with his congregation, who would often respond by clapping and making comments during the reading of Scripture and the sermon. "St. Augustine was known to ask questions of the people present if he wanted to impress upon them the importance of what he was saying. In his De Doctrina Christian 4, 39, he explicitly advocated this practice. While preaching a sermon in Carthage, for example, he said, Now all say after me, 'Charity from a pure heart.' Then all his listeners repeated the phrase after him. Often the people would voice their approval or disapproval of what Augustine said by shouting acclamations or beating their breasts, for example, when Augustine spoke of the need for contribution."[16]

This form of sermon dialogue passed out of existence during

---

14. William D. Thomson and Gordon C. Bennett, *Dialogue Preaching* (Valley Forge: Judson Press, 1969), p. 17.

15. Ibid.

16. Ibid.

the early middle ages because of the increasing formalization of church worship. So when the Reformation arrived, the Reformers did not feel inclined to reintroduce it to the Church and to give this kind of opportunity to the congregations under their care. For this reason Reformed churches have been reluctant to change the time-honored tradition of the monologue sermonic presentation being made by one minister alone, with no discussion following.

As a new congregation, the Westminster Fellowship felt it was on the right track when it discovered through reading that this dialogue form of preaching encouraged many progressively minded churchmen throughout the world to experiment. Many influences have wetted the appetite of less tradition-bound Christians to consider this as a possibility for their services. "The current theological emphasis of a valid encounter with the world, experimentation with new means of reaching the secular generation with the gospel, the opportunities for ecumenical relationships, along with the contribution of group dynamics, psychology and communication theory"[17] have been instrumental in opening up the possibility of many churches utilizing the dialogue sermon.

The Westminster Fellowship discovered that following Vatican Council, the Archdiocese of Australia had recommended to its pastors that "it would be better to present the sermons in a dialogue form rather than in the classical manner of preacher to people."[18] *Time* magazine commented on this new form of presentation in an article on May 17, 1968.

> Today, more and more U.S. clergymen are letting the people in the pew talk back, experimenting with dialogue sermons as an alternate to the pulpit monologue. One reason for this communal approach to the exposition of God's Word is that today's educated congregations are unwilling to put up with the authoritative preaching that lacks the stamp of credibility. Advocates of the dialogue sermon point out that since industry,

---

17. Ibid., p. 23.
18. Ibid., p. 7.

government, and education have discovered the virtue of the seminar and the conference, the church should also explore this avenue of intellectual discovery.[19]

Also, the World Council of Churches had made pronounce- ments at its meeting in Uppsala, Sweden, in 1968 to the effect "that the churches have traditionally known the power of the preached word to convince men of the call of God in their situation . . . yet in our day, the sermon as prepared and preached by one man comes increasingly under question. In these circumstances, the traditional sermon ought to be sup- plemented by new means of proclamation."[20]

The Westminster Fellowship and its pastor and officers began to feel that this form had significance for them. They were not concerned, as *Time* magazine reported, to institute this method of preaching merely to satisfy their intellectual inquiry after truth. Nor were they stimulated by the secular world's desire to dialogue in seminars and conferences, although they knew that the small group discussion at conferences was particularly helpful. They simply wanted their church worship to come alive with the Spirit's reality; and they were convinced that this method, if dedicated to the Lord, could be used to bring this about.

Several things must be considered if this is to happen in the local church. The pastor should attempt to prepare his sermons and then discuss them with a worship committee before they are preached. This would involve qualified lay people in the preparation of the sermon, as well as in the designing of questions that emerge out of the sermon. Some pastors have utilized this form to "reduce their extensive study so that [they] would not have to slave over a hot typewriter for hours," but the pastor of the Westminster Fellowship was not concerned with shortening the time of preparation but with involving the people more in an encounter with the Word of God. He felt that if the office bearers of the church and other responsible

---

19. Ibid.
20. Ibid., p. 8.

people in the Fellowship were involved in preparing the sermon, they would be used in getting "the ball rolling" and others would follow suit. The committee cautioned the pastor against a few of the pitfalls of his profession when leading a discussion. He was advised not to make a comment or preach a minor sermon after every response made by the congregation. He was not to be anxious if there was no immediate response to his questions. People need time to think about what they want to say and might not just talk "off the top of their heads." He needed to exercise restraint in not summing up all biblical subjects with a kind of *ex cathedra* position, as though he were the final authority. He should recommend books to read for follow-up and additional passages of Scripture for home study.

As the Westminster Fellowship embarked upon this dialogue approach, the congregation quickly responded, and soon it was an integral part of their worship. Often after a sermon was preached and questions were asked, people related how their own insights had been deepened and in what way, how they were corrected with respect to some preconceived notion that had not been tested by Scripture. People also confessed a renewal of their faith and an ability to retain throughout the week the sermon that had been preached because it had been discussed in this way. The dialogue form was engaged in congregationally, but increasingly they found that people opened up more effectively if they were divided into small groups for discussion. Because of the seating arrangement for the services, they were able to get people to move their chairs together in groups of four or five. This gave everyone an opportunity to articulate his response. It was generally felt that the sermon became more pertinent to life's issues than ever before, and the pastor was able to overcome the feeling he often had that his sermons might as well have been written from the moon—they contained so little mention of his immediate surroundings and revealed so little knowledge of ordinary folks' actual difficulties.[21]

---

21. David MacLennan, *Pastoral Preaching* (Philadelphia: The Westminster Press, 1954), p. 29.

Another suitable medium for suitable scriptural presentation that needs incorporation into Christian worship is drama. This has been a form used by the Church for many centuries but not very widely in Protestant churches. The medieval church created the "mystery plays" in order to instruct the illiterate. In modern times the Christian film industry has been used by the Lord to present many biblical truths in dramatic form, based either upon biblical scenes or contemporary situations.

Not too many churches have embarked upon this dramatic presentation of truth, because it takes a group of qualified people to engage in this undertaking. However, if a team of actors could be trained, they could meet together for the study of certain scriptural passages that could be creatively acted out. These presentations, used on suitable occasions, can be very helpful in relating the message of God's Word to daily life. When followed by helpful questions and discussion, people are compelled to grapple with some of the issues of life that are often ignored. To see the value of dramatizations "places the truth in such an imaginative form that people respond through several of their senses. For the preacher it means presenting the gospel in such a way that the people will respond to it with their whole being—they virtually participate in the gospel itself. When a preacher presents the gospel in a dramatic form and the congregation react together, the sermon becomes a shared experience in which all are vital participants in the drama unfolding before their eyes."[22]

"The preaching of the word must also be integrally linked to the *reading of scripture*. At the Reformation the reading of the Bible was followed upon with a prayer of God's illumination of His Word and then the sermon."[23] There was no separation between these two events. The Church, which is being renewed in faith, must have a desire to hear the Word of God in a manner that stimulates deeper commitment. If the passage for

---

22. Ronald Sleeth, *Persuasive Preaching* (New York: Harper and Row, 1956), pp. 66–67.
23. James Hastings Nicols, *Corporate Worship in the Reformed Tradition* (Richmond: John Knox Press, 1968).

the sermon could be printed in the church bulletin and read by the entire congregation, it would be much more meaningful as an act of worship. This helps people to see the Word and to read it in a version common to all. One of the most edifying aspects of the worship of the Westminster Fellowship was the use of Leslie Brandt's little volumes on the Psalms, which were particularly appreciated because they spoke the language of modern man. These volumes, *Good Lord, Where Are You?* and *God is Here, Let's Celebrate*, express the truth of the psalmist's experience in a most contemporary and yet poetically beautiful way. These are most effective when read collectively.

*Language.* The important thing in the reading of Scripture, along with the preaching of a sermon (using both dialogue and drama), is the kind of language used. The Reformation was concerned that every man hear the gospel in his own tongue, and so Latin was abandoned. But, unfortunately, Protestants, through the use of the Authorized Version (1611) perpetuated an archaic religious vocabulary that often reduces the reality of vital communication. We should be grateful that today there has been a breaking away from these outmoded forms of expression and a concerted effort to relate to people meaningfully, both young and old. "Speech must be varied and the message constantly modified and changed in the form in which it is delivered."[24] Whether the Church should go as far as Dietrich Bonhoffer, who wanted Christians to discover a nonreligious vocabulary set free from all churchly jargon, is something we have yet to settle. We certainly know that religious terminology has often been a stumbling block for the unchurched, and so Bonhoffer's prophecy may be forced upon us for acceptance: "The day will come when men are called to speak God's Word in such a way as to transform and renew the world. There will be a new language perhaps, completely unreligious, but which will liberate and redeem like the words of Jesus, so that men are shocked but still convinced of its power."[25] Certainly the

---

24. Hans–Joachim Kraus, *The Threat and the Power* (Richmond: John Knox Press, 1966), p. 79.
25. Ibid., p. 80.

Church must be ready to do this, if in so doing it leads many of the unchurched masses to accept the claims of Christ upon their lives. The Westminster Fellowship's attempts to do this were made through the use of modern versions of Scripture and language reasonably free from Christian "in" terminology. This was necessary because the ministry of the Fellowship involved them with many unchurched, alcoholics from AA, and disenchanted youth. Marshall McLuhan has commented that "God may use many ways to get His truth across to people."[26] Reformed congregations that want to feel the impact of God's creative Spirit upon them need to be involved in any legitimate form of presentation of the gospel, through Scripture reading and preaching, that will not only build up God's people but will also draw the lost of our society to him.

---

## Chapter 4 (A)

Calvin, John. *The Institutes of the Christian Religion*. Philadelphia: The Westminster Press, 1959.

Killinger, John. *Experimental Preaching*. Nashville: Abingdon Press, 1973.

Killinger, John. *The Centrality of Preaching in the Total Task of the Ministry*. Waco, Texas: Word Books, 1969.

Kraus, Hans-Joachim. *The Threat and the Power*. Richmond: John Knox Press, 1966.

MacLennan, David. *Pastoral Preaching*. Philadelphia: The Westminster Press, 1954.

Malcomson, William M. *The Preaching Event*. Philadelphia: The Westminster Press, 1968.

McLuhan, Marshall. *Understanding Media – The Extensions of Man*. New York: McGraw-Hill, 1964.

---

26. Marshall McLuhan, *Understanding Media – The Extensions of Man* (New York: McGraw-Hill, 1964), p. 11.

Morrow, Thomas M. *Worship and Preaching*. London: Epworth Press, 1956.

Nicols, James Hastings. *Corporate Worship in the Reformed Tradition*. Richmond: John Knox Press, 1968.

Sleeth, Ronald. *Persuasive Preaching*. New York: Harper and Row, 1956.

Thompson, William D. and Bennett, Gordon C. *Dialogue Preaching*. Valley Forge: Judson Press, 1969.

---

## (B) *The Involvement of the Laity in Praise*

Music, praise, and prayer play an enormous role in the expression of renewal. Those who experience the reshaping of their Christian life through the release of God's Spirit find that through praise and prayer they are better able to demonstrate what is taking place in their lives. It has been said that "every revival of religion has been heralded and generated by prayer groups,"[1] and the Westminster Fellowship saw this revival happening to them as a congregation because of the new desire to praise God and to pray.

The prayer meeting of the Fellowship in previous days had been like most church mid-week meetings, essentially a Bible study with little or no singing. But this fresh desire to praise God in song was reminiscent of the days of the Reformation, "which expressed its renewal, not only in a resurgence of biblical preaching, but also in congregational singing."[2] The prayer meeting had been gradually degenerating into a static religious experience, with prayer being offered in a flat, perfunctory manner, engaged in because, despite everything, they did believe in prayer. Suddenly, under the impact of the Spirit, they began to be a living organism in terms of vital worship and intercession. There are some who imagine that it is only in beautifully appointed sanctuaries that uplifting worship can be

---

1. George Butterick, *Prayer* (Nashville: Abingdon Press, 1942), p. 272.

2. Dwight Seere, *Music in Protestant Worship* (Richmond: John Knox Press, 1972), p. 142.

offered effectively. Someone has commented "a theatre type auditorium is not conducive to worship, but enter a cathedral, we instinctively have a desire to be hushed and commune with God."[3] This was a point of view that many in the Fellowship had held, but they began to discover how erroneous it was as far as church renewal is concerned. At this particular time, the prayer meeting was being held in a recreation room of a home, and in that kind of atmosphere they were finding a depth of worship that had not been part of their Christian life, even though they were worshiping in a sanctuary that was aesthetically pleasing.

When the Westminster Fellowship came into existence as a new congregation, they were compelled to examine themselves critically as a Reformed church, because God was active in their lives in a new way. They needed to evaluate what was happening to them. The liturgical renewal that was taking place in many churches had made them "realize that one of the tokens of liturgical renewal is dissatisfaction with what is merely traditional and a corresponding desire to discover what riches may be available from other traditions."[4] They had been driven to ask what there was to learn from other church traditions, particularly in the light of Paul's words to the Corinthians, "All things are yours" (1 Cor. 3:31). This resulted in an enrichment that began to deepen their spiritual lives immeasurably. This did not keep them, however, from examining their own tradition of both Scripture and church history, seeking to understand what they had to say to Christians who were not of the Reformed tradition. They felt it would be wrong to wipe out certain aspects of their heritage simply because they were a new church. It was known that the early Christians had a Jewish background, which manifested itself increasingly as a charismatic fellowship, moving toward a more structured type of service, as the Didache (A.D. 100) reveals. Early Christians

3. F. Lee Whittlesley, *A Comprehensive Program of Church Music* (Philadelphia: The Westminster Press, 1947), p. 136.

4. Ronald C.D. Jasper, ed. *The Renewal of Worship* (New York, Toronto: Oxford University Press, 1965), p. 63.

did not neglect some of the richness of their heritage, even though there was a breaking out of new expressions of worship. As the Westminster Fellowship grew in structure and understanding of what it wanted to be, they found themselves moving away from some aspects of worship previously used and toward expressions of worship that enlivened their services considerably.

They began to move away from (1) aesthetically beautiful services, (2) the experience-centered hymns of traditional hymnody, and (3) gospel music.

*Aesthetic Services.* Beautiful music, which has developed through the history of Christian worship, may have a place in the life of the Church today. But sometimes it is so highly sophisticated that it does not always communicate meaningfully to people of less-developed musical tastes. It is unfortunate that some liturgists are governed by secular, rather than spiritual, standards when it comes to evaluating the quality of a service. Some have become so "churchy" in their appreciation of what they think constitutes a worshipful service that they ignore the fact that "it is not for us to say what God is able to use for His purpose. If God was once worshipped in David's strange dance . . . if the esoteric speaking in tongues of the Corinthian church was judged by Paul to have a place in the Christian community, then surely all things human, no matter how crude, are within God's sovereignty and in His mysterious grace can be used to His praise."[5] Eric Routley, a musicologist of high taste concurs with this insight when he writes in his book on church music.

> Examination of principles that made church music "churchy" and made it especially churchy where the church was most firmly entrenched in bourgeois exclusiveness, has led to the discovery that half of them did not exist and the other half were impatient of much modification. When Saul's daughter rebuked David for his dance of joy she stood for the essential shockableness of conventional religion for the "nothing in

---

5. Paul W. Hoon, *The Integrity of Worship* (Nashville: Abingdon Press, 1971), p. 38.

excess" decorum of popular piety. And David said that this is superstition. Responsible musicians are far from sure that we have rightly stated the truth about musical beauty in what we have assumed for generations.[6]

The Westminster Fellowship wanted worship to be a beautiful experience but in the spirit of holiness, and not necessarily by standards set by the world. It did not mean that they rejected classical music entirely, for on occasions it was felt appropriate. They simply felt that choir music needed to fit into the context of the service much more than in the past, and they did not hesitate to say to their choir director that "anthems must be of worthy texts that can inspire the soul, enlighten the mind, and express the finest emotions of the congregation."[7] The Fellowship believed that "the best anthems will be durable, simple in motive, worshipful and will help us to return to the function of which Martin Luther states, 'putting music upon the living and holy Word of God wherewith to praise and honor the same, so that the beautiful ornament of music brought back to its right use, may serve its blessed Maker and His Christian people.' "[8] This means that those who volunteer to sing in the choir must present the kind of music that will be spiritually uplifting to the whole church and must not attempt productions that are beyond the people. A choir that is spiritually divorced only makes choir music "an element of comedy, sometimes tragedy and even a farce."[9]

*Instrumental Music.* When it comes to the matter of instrumental music in the church service, some people have been accustomed to the organ alone. It seems disrespectful to them to introduce the modern instruments of the guitar, trumpet, saxophone, and other instruments that appear on the surface to

---

6. Eric Routley, *Church Music and Modern Times* (New York, Toronto: Oxford University Press, 1969), p. 212.

7. Arthur C. Lovelace and William C. Rice, *Music in the Worship of the Church* (Nashville: Abingdon Press, 1960), p. 130.

8. Ibid., p. 130.

9. Robert M. Stevenson, *Return of Protestant Music* (Durham: Duke University Press, 1953, p. 120.

have no place in the services of divine worship. But everyone in the church should be given an opportunity to express his gift, and many young people have the ability to play these instruments. They must be willing to do so for the glory of God and not merely to make the services more contemporary in character. We should not ignore this desire on the basis of aesthetic taste. In fact, as we come to the Bible, we will see that some of these instruments were used in the temple worship (Ps. 150). Presbyterian and Reformed services have been somewhat negative when it comes to the use of musical instruments in church worship, basing their understanding upon principles expressed by John Calvin. As we study some of the statements made by this great Reformer on the use of instrumental music, we see that his interpretations are quite arbitrary and often inconsistent with other things he commented upon in the Old Testament. Commenting on 1 Samuel 18:1, he wrote, "It would be too ridiculous to believe oneself to be offering God a more noble service using organs. . . . Instrument music was tolerated in the time of the Law because the people were then in infancy. . . . All that is needed is a simple and pure singing of the divine praises coming from the heart and mouth and in the vulgar tongue."[10] He also continues in the same vein when he comments on Psalm 92: "The Levites were appointed to the office of singers and called upon to employ their instruments of music, not as if this were in itself necessary only it was useful as an elementary aid to the people of God in ancient times, and now that Christ has appeared and the Church has reached full age, it were only to bury the light of the Gospel should we introduce the shadows of a departed dispensation."[11] Reformed churches, up until the late nineteenth century, banned musical instruments on the basis of this kind of argument. We should be grateful that recently Reformed Christians have restored the organ to church worship, but why have we stopped with this

---

10. John Calvin, *Commentary on 1 Samuel* (Grand Rapids: William B. Eerdman's, 1970), p. 370.
11. John Calvin, *Commentary on the Psalms*, (Philadelphia: The Westminster Press, 1947) pp. 494–95.

instrument, as if it were the only one that God has given to the Church? We should welcome the restoration of musical instruments—incorporating orchestras into our praise, if possible. This enables those who play an instrument to become more personally involved in the ministry of music. We should not hesitate to use some of the new songs that have been written, because they are not only popular in style but often present the Word of God in a fashion that captivates the heart.

The music of the synagogue was the music of the people. "The synagogue music was folk in nature, in contrast to the elaborate musical system of the temple. This folk music had been handed down from generation to generation, undergoing changes to fit the particular era or group of people. Religious folk music was representative of the emotions of the worshipers rather than being merely a part of a rigid ritual . . ., the use of the different folk melodies shown in the Psalm titles relates even the Book of Psalms into the category of folk religion."[12] It was a joy for the Westminster Fellowship to discover that the contemporary tunes accompanying some of the Psalms of the Bible put us in biblical tradition, perhaps more than those which were dedicated to the use of high-brow music of the European church of the seventeenth and eighteenth centuries.

*Experience-Centered Hymns Versus Objective Hymns of Praise.* In the spiritual growth of the Westminster Fellowship there was a gradual turning away from experience-centered hymns to more objective praise hymns. Many of the traditionally beloved hymns of the Church are very experience centered; and although there is a place for this kind of music, it should be subordinated to the more exalted hymns of praise to God. As a congregation is renewed in the Spirit, a strong desire for praise makes itself felt, magnifying God for his redemptive work in Jesus Christ. Hymns of Christian experience, while not altogether dropped by the members of the Fellowship, were given less and less place in the service. This was not by the personal or arbitrary choice of the pastor but of the people as

---

12. William Lloyd Hooper, *Church Music in Transition* (Nashville: Broadman Press, 1963), p. 20.

they requested certain hymns to sing. There is a great need for Christians to discover, with Evelyn Underhill, that "the tendency to decline from adoration to demand, and from supernatural to the ethical, shows how strong a pull is needed to neutralize the anthropocentric trend in the human mind."[13] People grow in spiritual depth when they request those hymns which are centered more upon the praise of God in all of his redeeming acts rather than those hymns which express human desires. Congregations, rather than choir masters or pastors, must see themselves as the selectors of praise, according to 1 Corinthians 14:26; and as they assume this responsibility, if their lives are being renewed in the Spirit, they will choose hymns that will be predominantly praise in nature.

*The Gospel Song.* The Westminster Fellowship also found themselves turning away from the so-called gospel song and to the use of Scripture prepared for singing. Many of the gospel hymn tunes are too sentimental in character and unexpressive for the words that have been composed. The use of Scripture in praise became a very expressive means by which the Fellowship offered its praise to God. Many of these psalm melodies have been recently produced and "provided us with the wings of faith for the church in its corporate praise."[14] The use of Scripture gives a deeper appreciation for the Word, not only as medium through which the sermon comes but also as a channel through which praise may be offered. With its roots in the Reformed tradition, the Westminster Fellowship had used the psalms of the 1650 Psalter, usually one at each service. But now there was a renewed interest in the use of psalms, and they were grateful that new compositions had been prepared. The tunes are modern in style but very conducive to the spirit of praise. Often the entire selection of hymns would be based upon the psalms, and this gave us a deep sense of being joined with our fathers in the Reformation, for whom this kind of hymn was customary.

As the Fellowship moved away from some former patterns, they discovered that hymns of praise are one of the most im-

---

13. Evelyn Underhill, *Worship* (New York: Harper and Row, 1936), p. 17.

14. Thomas M. Kerr, *The Word in Worship* (New York, Toronto: Oxford University Press, 1962), p. 99.

portant aspects of the worship of God. They found it difficult to understand why they had been so limited in the amount of singing they had done in church previously. Usually three, and sometimes four, hymns had been sung in the past. What had motivated the Church to be so limited in praise? They discovered that prior to the Reformation, Pope Gregory in the sixth century banned people's musical participation and thus "turned the Church's song into a monkish preserve for a well nigh millenium."[15] When the Reformation came along, this attitude was not overcome immediately. Luther was the most musical of the Reformers, but Zwingli eliminated sung praise entirely from the services in Strassburg. Calvin, after observing what was happening in Strassburg, brought the singing of psalms alone into the worship services of Geneva.[16] Some have accused him of being the "enemy of music"[17] or "personally opposed to the use of any kind of music, bowing slightly to popular pressure when he permitted the singing of biblical texts,"[18] but this kind of opinion cannot be sustained. A much more competent scholar has written,

> When he [Calvin] was exiled from Geneva, 1538 to 1541, he discovered the popularity and influence of a well known composer Marot whose psalm tunes he approved. After surveying the situation he drew up his Essentials of a Well Ordered Church, in which he gave prominence to psalm singing for three reasons. 1) The example of the ancient church and Paul, 2) the spiritual benefit to prayer, and 3) because the Pope had deprived the church of the benefit found in the psalms by having them mumbled unintelligibly. On his return to Geneva Calvin required the singing of Psalms to be part of the public worship and was so successful in establishing psalm singing that in 1559 the Synod of the Reformed Churches of France decreed that every member should bring his own psalter to worship.[19]

---

15. Ibid., p. 98.

16. William Rice, *A Concise History of Church Music* (Nashville: Abingdon Press, 1964).

17. Stevenson, *Return of Protestant Music*, p. 21.

18. Hooper, *Church Music in Transition*, pp. 46, 48.

19. Henry C. Horn, *O Sing Unto the Lord* (Philadelphia: Fortress Press, 1956), p. 3.

We should be grateful that, in the charismatic renewal of the Church in the twentieth century, psalms are being restored, as well as other hymns. This leads us to the question, If praise is such an important aspect of worship, why should it not be given a considerable period of time for expression and not be subordinated to the sermon? Some Christians feel, with the Quakers, that "our lives can be lifted to God's truth and love in other ways."[20] It is true that we are not necessarily worshiping in spirit and truth, even if we use some of the greatest hymns of the Church or contemporary expressions of praise. Christian singing must emerge from the heart as well as from the voice, because "religious music without religion is almost always vulgar and dull."[21] Scripture encourages Christians to sing psalms, hymns, and spiritual songs, singing and making melody in our *hearts* to the Lord (Ep. 5:18, Col. 3:16).

Because man is not only a rational being gifted with powers of reason but also an emotional being, we must accept the fact that music arouses this aspect of his nature and makes it a medium through which genuine worship can be offered. The Westminster Fellowship discovered that just to sing one hymn and then move on to another part of the service was not adequate in helping them express the worshipful desires of their hearts. The spirit, when renewed by the Holy Spirit, longs to worship God (Ps. 42:1), and thus the Fellowship began to engage in praise for at least thirty or forty minutes, interspersed with prayers of thanksgiving. This lifting up of the emotions in song had a profound effect upon the congregation and enabled them at times to be so filled with "wonder, love, and praise" that they often moved into the Holy Communion service because it seemed to be the most fitting thing to do. As a result of this kind of exaltation, they were better able to appreciate the significance of the sacrament as it communicated God's love to them. The congregation testified to the quickening of their love for the Lord in a new way.

Emotions, of course, must be controlled. Some evangelical Christians often become overly emotional in their services, and

---

20. Ibid.
21. Kerr, *The Word in Worship*, p. 92.

attempts are often made to use music to manipulate people. Music can become a dangerous thing if not controlled in the spirit of love. We can understand why some of the early Church fathers were fearful of music when it was not used properly. Augustine, for example, writes, "At times I seem to give them [church melodies] more honor than is seemly, feeling our minds to be more holily and fervently raised unto a flame of devotion by the holy words themselves when thus sung."[22] Music must be under the control of the Spirit, just like everything else in the service; and emotions must be held together with the other parts of man's nature. Jesus' words are very pertinent: "Thou shalt love the Lord thy God with all thy heart, and with all thy soul, and with all thy strength and with all thy mind" (Matt. 22:37). This is particularly true of the heart and soul when praise is being offered to God in song. The emotions are not easily quickened, any more than the temperature of a thermometer rises quickly. It needs continued heat under it in order to lift its temperature. In the same way, the emotional life of the Christian needs a stimulant to lift it to the place of purposeful praise. Many church members will testify that merely singing one hymn at the beginning of a service means little or nothing to them. People come to the service often with the thoughts of the morning upon their minds, and the singing of one hymn at the commencement of the service is overclouded by their thoughts of other things.

In the Westminster Fellowship it was discovered that singing needed to be more lengthy, thus enabling the Spirit to turn the mind away from the thoughts of the world and to the Lord himself. "The emotions were stirred and the imagination began to relate sounds to mental pictures,"[23] particularly the image and reality of Jesus Christ. This aspect of worship must not be ignored if there is to be renewal in the Church. Music is not an end in itself, nor a means to pep the people up for the coming of the all-important sermon. Singing of praise stands in its own right as an act of worship and thus deserves to be engaged in

---

22. Ibid.
23. Robert M. Stevenson, *Patterns of Protestant Church Music* (Durham: Duke University Press, 1953), p. 19.

with fervor and enthusiasm. The utilization of psalms, Scripture, and other hymns is one of the most significant ways for a congregation to be lifted in praise. It is in this mood of praise that the shorter Catechism's injunction can be experienced: "Man's chief end is to glorify God and enjoy Him forever" (question 1). If God is to be enjoyed, then time must be taken for the full benefit of this aspect of worship to be felt by the worshiper.

*Singing in the Spirit.* Another aspect of praise that was restored to the worship of the Westminster Fellowship is known as "singing in the Spirit." The apostle Paul speaks of this phenomena in his letter to the Corinthians where he refers to his own personal experience, "I will sing with my spirit and I will sing with my understanding also" (1 Cor. 14:15). The Fellowship came to understand this as a free, spontaneous offering of sung praise, which might emerge at any given point in the act of worship. When a congregation does not rush from one hymn to another but often sits quietly contemplating the words just sung, it may be an occasion for someone in the congregation to start leading in a free song that has no written musical composition and no intelligible words. Often those who spoke in tongues would utilize their prayer language to join in this kind of praise. Rather than producing a cacophony of sound as all these various melodies were sung at once, the Spirit would create a unified song, full of diversity, harmonious and ethereal. It had the effect of lifting up the spirit to God in an incomparable way and with such intensity as to release the gift of prophecy.

There is no way that this kind of praise can be structured, but if it breaks forth at the appropriate moment, it must be in keeping with the mood of the service. It may express itself several times during a service, although there may be times when it will not manifest itself. In the Fellowship, those who did not sing in tongues would often offer to the Lord some word of gratitude, composing a poetic expression, with melody, which would be offered to the Lord. This phenomena is not easy to describe, but it is one way in which this Reformed congregation, moving in the charismatic dimension, entered more fully into a type of worship that they felt was characteristic of the early Church.

*Conclusion.* Whenever the priesthood of all believers is taken seriously by the pastor, so that he believes that the whole congregation is called to offer praise to God, he will allow the Spirit to call forth a response in sung praise, which is not experienced usually by churches today. The truth of William Barkley's words needs to be rediscovered by the Christian leaders of worship: "The really notable thing about the early church service must have been that almost everyone came feeling that he had both the privilege and the obligation of contributing to it. A man did not come only to receive, but also to give."[24]

## Chapter 4 (B)

Barkley, William. *The Letter to the Corinthians.* Philadelphia: The Westminster Press, 1959.

Butterick, George. *Prayer.* Nashville: Abingdon Press, 1942.

Calvin, John. *Commentary on Psalms*, Vol. 3. Edinburgh, 1947

Calvin, John. *Commentary on the Psalms*, Vol. 3. Philadelphia: The Westminster Press, 1947.

Calvin, John. *Commentary on 1 Samuel.* Grand Rapids: William B. Eerdman's, 1970.

Hoon, Paul H. *The Integrity of Worship.* Nashville: Abingdon Press, 1971.

Hooper, William Lloyd. *Church Music in Transition.* Nashville: Broadman Press, 1963.

Horn, Henry C. *O Sing Unto the Lord.* Philadelphia: Fortress Press, 1956.

Jasper, Ronald C.D., ed. *The Renewal of Worship.* New York, Toronto: Oxford University Press, 1965.

Kerr, Thomas M. *The Word in Worship.* New York, Toronto: Oxford University Press, 1962.

Lovelace, Arthur C. and Rice, William C. *Music in the Worship of the Church.* Nashville: Abingdon Press, 1960.

24. William Barkley, *The Letter to the Corinthians* (Philadelphia: The Westminster Press, 1959), p. 150.

Rice, William. *A Concise History of Church Music*. Nashville: Abingdon Press, 1964.

Routley, Eric. *Church Music and Modern Times*. New York, Toronto: Oxford University Press, 1969.

Seere, Dwight. *Music in Protestant Worship*. Richmond: John Knox Press, 1972.

Stevenson, Robert M. *Return of Protestant Music*. Durham: Duke University Press, 1953.

Underhill, Evelyn. *Worship*. New York: Harper and Row, 1936.

Whittlesley, F. Lee. *A Comprehensive Program of Church Music*. Philadelphia: The Westminster Press, 1947.

---

## (C) *The Involvement of the Laity in Prayer*

In the area of prayer, a Spirit-led congregation needs to discover the truth of Elton Trueblood's words, that the Christian life is "essentially a life of private and public prayer." The movement away from certain fixed patterns and the adoption of new approaches to singing also need to be applied to prayer. The realization that we are a priesthood of believers enables a congregation to overcome the feeling that the pastor is called by God to be the chief intercessor in the service. In the new realization of their responsibility to engage in prayer, the Westminster Fellowship began to move away from (1) monologue prayer offered only by the pastor; (2) the long pastoral prayer, which encompasses all things, and (3) sermon-centered services to prayer-centered ones. As the prayer life of the congregation was remodeled, they moved toward new types of prayer, which involved everyone and were characterized by (1) congregational participation in all forms of prayer offered by the Christian community when gathered for worship, i.e., confessions, thanksgiving, intercession; (2) the adaptation of a more personal vocabulary; with the restoration of certain symbols of prayer found in the Bible and Christian tradition, such as kneeling and the lifting up of the hands.

The traditional Presbyterian service, in which the pastor

offers all the prayer, is no longer adequate for today's congregation. Monologue prayer should come to an end, and dialogue prayer should be introduced and encouraged. The long pastoral prayer has often given people the opportunity to tune out, because it is so tedious and covers too many subjects. Hearing the lone voice of the pastor tends to deaden the sense of being involved in prayer with him, and therefore the prayer that the church as a whole needs to offer is minimized. Most honest people confess that what they come to church for is to hear the sermon, and they regard the other aspects of church worship as irrelevant. The council of the Fellowship knew that this had to be changed. Instead of prayer being a spiritual exercise that eliminates the involvement of the people, the whole church must learn how to become participants in an active way.

Traditionally, many Presbyterian services have begun with some silence, preceded by such words of Scripture as "God is in His holy temple, let all the earth keep silence before Him" (Hab. 2:20), "Be still and know that I am God" (Ps. 46:10), "Come ye apart and rest awhile" (Matt. 14:13). However, not too much time has been spent in silence. The Westminster Fellowship began to do this with great spiritual profit. Before entering into some of the more active aspects of worship, the people were encouraged to accept this silence as a creative time, a time for casting their cares upon God, a time for setting aside worldly responsibilities, and a time for a resolved intention to reach out to God in love and praise. This time of silence should not, in their opinion, be musically accompanied, which is often a distraction rather than an assistance to prayer. Constant musical involvement by the organ or choir at every interval of worship confirms Paul Hoon's humorous words, "The participation in services in which, in addition to hymns, anthems, chants and postlude, every spare second is filled with music from the organ in the manner of Muzak, Muzak everywhere . . . betray sensitivity to proportion and cheapen meaning."[1]

---

1. Paul W. Hoon, *The Integrity of Worship* (Nashville: Abingdon Press, 1971), p. 280.

As the Westminster Fellowship prepared for worship in silence, a few passages of Scripture were read, and then silence followed. This helped to produce a reverent atmosphere and to quiet the soul, because most Protestants today are not accustomed to sitting quietly and waiting for a service to begin. Instead, they engage in constant conversation. Silence helps to make the transition from busy minds and talkativeness to a mood of worship. Prolonged silence of up to five minutes has the power to do this. As pastor, I had worshiped some years before with the Quakers at Earlham College, in Richmond, Indiana. The people who attended the nine o'clock service came to take part in a "solemn service of silence." The forty minutes or so of silence was so pregnated with the Spirit's presence that it was one of the most dynamic times of worship I had ever experienced. I prayed that it might happen in my congregation, and this request was granted.

*Forms of Prayer.* Throughout its long history, the Christian Church has utilized three basic forms of prayer: fixed, free, and extemporary. As a Reformed church not accustomed to fixed prayers, the Fellowship discovered that "liturgy can be used to describe all forms of corporate worship and those most addicted to set forms of prayer could not agree that their prayer is unrelated to the Holy Spirit."[2]

Written prayer is not necessarily a stereotyped ritual but can be a very creative act, depending upon how the worshiper approaches it. In opening prayers, selections from the psalms, litanies, or other liturgically prepared prayers which help to stimulate the minds of the worshipers toward God may be used. Some of the most helpful of these have been written in the modern idiom by Leslie Brandt—*Good Lord, Where Are You?* and *God is Here, Let's Celebrate.* There is a need on the part of most Protestants to overcome their prejudices with respect to reading prayers, especially when we realize that Calvin and Knox used written prayers in their services. There is also a need to go beyond the classical Puritan attitude expressed by John

---

2. Ronald C.D. Jasper, ed. *The Renewal of Worship* (New York: Oxford University Press, 1965), p. 58.

Owen, that written prayer is "the guilding of the poisonous pill whose operation, when it was swallowed, was to bereave men of their sense of reason and faith."[3] We must abandon the idea that reading prayers robs a minister of the gift of prayer and is only an accommodation to those who feel they cannot express themselves adequately in their own words. The Spirit is not necessarily quenched when written prayer is offered, as long as it is used in a creative way. It is unimaginative to read prayers in the exact same way, week by week; but written prayers, prepared on a weekly basis and inserted in the church bulletin for congregational use, can be a very helpful expression of Christian unity in prayer.

After opening the service with silent prayer or written prayers led by a member of the congregation, the fellowship engaged in the singing of hymns of adoration. Joyous worship of God in song should precede the offering of confessional prayer, because Paul's words are most applicable, "knowing that it is the goodness of God that leadeth thee to repentance" (Rom. 2:4). The great adoration hymns have a way of stimulating appreciation of God for who he is and for the salvation which he has offered us in Jesus Christ. With the emotion of gratitude aroused, participation in the prayers of confession can be much more realistic. The attitude of John Castell, which is so typical of most liturgical services, is not necessarily true: "In traditional liturgies, confession preceded the other acts of the service on the principle that until we have confessed and been forgiven we are not prepared for further communion with God."[4] The Westminster Fellowship discovered that worship of God through songs of adoration prepared the heart for a true confession.

*Confessional Prayer.* There are, of course, two ways to go about making public confession of sin. The pastor can either offer a general confession himself, which is either the same every Sunday, or varied week by week; or the congregation can corporately join in this confession. But can true confession,

---

3. Ibid., p. 60.
4. John Castell, *Rediscovering Prayer* (New York: Association Press, 1955), p. 68.

which touches the heart deeply, be made that does not center not only on the collective need of God's people to be forgiven but also upon the individual's need to feel the impact of God's grace upon his guilty spirit? The words of John Castell are certainly appropriate: "We must combine the large sweep of general confession with the unique and more particular needs of our individual lives. Such prayer will require a much more exhaustive effort than the utterance or repetition of general statements as to our sinfulness. We must bring ourselves to that inward surrender of self which will allow God to restore clarity and health to the interior life."[5] We also need to acknowledge the truth of Thomas Morrow's words: "There is little value in praying in vague, general terms for forgiveness, still less if a phrase is added on to the end of our prayers, and 'this we ask with the forgiveness of all our sins,' as a pious postscript. In confession we need to be definite and specific, even though this will of necessity exclude some sins and some needy people."[6]

How to help a congregation confess their sins personally is a great challenge. In the Westminster Fellowship we invited people to ask the Holy Spirit to make them aware of anything in their lives that needed to be forgiven. This was followed by silence as people searched their hearts, listening to the voice of the Spirit recalling things that needed to be confessed.

Sometimes this desire to be freed from the burden of sin can be symbolized by something reminiscent of the scapegoat in the wilderness. Provide people with slips of paper, and ask them to write down their sins. Then these can be gathered up and brought to the chancel to a large wooden cross and left there, accompanied by words of absolution, which those who have truly repented and confessed their sins need to hear. This helps people to take their personal sins seriously, as well as those sins which congregations have participated in on a social level. No service should be exactly the same in this respect, "because new temptations and new wants should be taken up within our

---

5. Ibid., p. 69.

6. Thomas M. Morrow, *Worship and Preaching* (London: Epworth Press, 1956), p. 22.

prayers, and new sins confessed, and it is not to be thought that these can be well provided for in any prescribed composition."[7]

It can be a very significant act to follow this confession by giving the sign of peace to one another, because the sins that so often alienate us from God are sins that we have committed against members of our families or members of the church, and there is need for reconciliation. Healing and forgiveness on the horizontal level are just as important as on the vertical level with God.

*Prayers of Thanksgiving.* The service in the Westminster Fellowship often continued with joyful hymns of thanksgiving for the mercy and grace of God. After one has accepted the forgiveness of God, he can sing with deep feeling, "Amazing Grace, How Sweet the Sound," "Marvelous Grace of Our Loving Lord," or other hymns of this type. When the congregation came to offering prayers of thanksgiving led by the pastor or one of the leaders, the people were stimulated in a number of ways to express their gratitude. Sometimes a written prayer, or a series of spontaneous prayers, might be offered by the leader. This helped to stir the imagination. People would then speak forth their single word of thanksgiving for everything that had happened to them. We know that many people have been helped by Merlin Carothers's book *Power Through Praise* and have realized that everything in life provides us with a reason for gratitude. "In everything give thanks, for this is the will of God in Christ Jesus concerning you" (1 Thess. 4:3, 5:18). Gratitude must be associated with every experience in life. "In Christian prayer, there is a place for offering spontaneous thanks on every occasion of joy and every impulse to express gratitude . . . to give thanks in this deep and reverent way indicates that we must accept the whole of life with reverent joy as a gift from God."[8]

This means that people should be encouraged to speak forth the gratitude of their hearts not only for happy things but also

7. Isaac Watts, *Guide to Prayer, 1810*, Vol. 4, p. 27, quoted in Jasper, *Renewal of Worship*, p. 69.

8. Castell, *Rediscovering Prayer*, p. 88.

for the struggles of life, the delays to prayer, the hurts and sorrows of the heart. These times of open acknowledgment of gratitude can have a profound effect upon a congregation, binding them together as a church family as they learn to rejoice with those who rejoice and to weep with those who weep. The spirit of thanksgiving is much more than centering upon the favorable aspects of life; it also focuses upon the difficult, demanding experiences that make up our common life. When this is done in a service, the recitation of the De Teum or one of the great praise psalms (Ps. 103; 96; 116) can be most meaningful.

*Intercessory Prayer.* In the Westminster Fellowship intercessory prayer was offered as the climax to the service. After the sermon was preached, considerable time was spent in praying for God's blessing upon the world, the church, and those who specified their need for prayer. As much time was given for this as was taken for the sermon, and it was without doubt one of the richest times in the service. It is so important for Christians to discover that

> corporate prayer is the heart of corporate worship. Ritual is not central, however vital. Scripture is not central, for however indispensable and radiant, it is scriptural—that which is written, the record, the experience of the very Word, but not the Presence. Preaching is not central, for preaching, however inevitable and kindling, is still preaching—the heralding, not the very Lord Himself. When the rite is made central, prayer may become an incantation. When the Book is made central, prayer may become an appendage. When preaching is made central, prayer, as in Zwingli's order of service, may become only an introduction and conclusion to the service. The heart of religion is prayer—the uplifting of the hands, the speaking of human lips, the expectant waiting in silence. Prayer must go through the rite, the scripture, the symbolism, the sermon, as light through a window."[9]

It will be revolutionary for a Reformed church to take seriously the words of Frank Laubach: "Evangelical Christianity

---

9. Frank Butterick, *Prayer* (Nashville: Abingdon Press, 1942), p. 283.

is lost unless it discovers that the center and power of its divine service is prayer, not sermons."[10]

Intercession should begin with prayers for the world, because all too often Christians are nearsighted and concerned only with their own needs and desires. Often when we pray "we hardly enter into the presence of God before we bring out our shopping lists and inform God what we want. We treat Him as a means to our ends."[11] Sometimes the newspaper should be taken into the pulpit and certain news items read out, accompanied with either verbal or silent prayer. The same thing can be done for the work of the Church. It is not possible to pray for everything that has to do with the life of the Church, because "we should no more try to include everything and everybody in one prayer than we should try to include all truth in one sermon."[12] Sunday by Sunday a wide range of Christian concerns should be presented to the congregation for prayer, thus enabling the congregation to identify with as many human problems as possible. Above all, it is necessary to pray for the Church, which is suffering for its faith in many places, especially when some information has been read, which helps people to grasp some of the anguish through which the Church passes.

When personal needs were presented for prayer, the Fellowship was encouraged to be brief in its presentation. If a person wanted special ministry, they were invited to come forward for the laying on of hands. One of the ways the priesthood of all believers can be recognized is for the pastor to invite all who wish to join with him in this ancient act of "laying on of hands" to come forward. This gives the person prayed for a wonderful sense of being surrounded not only by the love of God but also by the love of Christ coming through his people.

One of the best methods for intercessory prayer, which involves the whole church, is to break the congregation into small

10. Frank Laubach, *Prayer* (Westwood, New Jersey: Fleming and Revell, 1946), p. 49.

11. Charles F. Wiston, *Pray* (Grand Rapids: William B. Eerdman's, 1972), p. 102.

12. Morrow, *Worship and Preaching*, p. 22.

groups. Everyone in the group is prayed for, as they request, and this helps the more timid members of the church to feel part of the prayer life of the congregation. This has not yet happened in the Westminster Fellowship, but it needs to be incorporated.

Another thing Christian people need to be encouraged to do is to carry a little intercessory notebook so that the names of people needing prayer can be recorded. Then, when the congregation gathers, these can be offered up. It must be admitted "that we do not need to inform the Lord about every person . . . the Lord already knows full well. We don't need to compose a prayer for each person on the list. In fifteen minutes we may easily and without haste pray for several hundred people."[13]

Intercessory prayer is an opportunity through which congregations that believe in the full expression of the gifts of the Spirit can manifest the gift of tongues. In the ministry of prayer, how little we realize the full depths of a person's need, let alone that of the world or the church. The weakness of which Paul spoke often overtakes us, "likewise the Spirit also helps our infirmities for we know not how to pray as we ought, but the Spirit himself intercedes for us with sighs too deep for words, and he searches the hearts of men and knows what is the mind of the Spirit, because the Spirit intercedes for the saints according to the will of God" (Rom. 8:26–27). F.F. Bruce, in his commentary on this passage in Romans, suggests that this is a reference to the gift of tongues, although it may include other forms of intercession.[14] Many have found by experience that it does.

Intercessory prayer reveals how limited is our understanding of human need and our capacity to express it. Even though the Reformers did not exercise the gift of tongues, they certainly understood the need of the Spirit to assist in the ministry of prayer. "In his lectures on Romans, Luther spoke with par-

---

13. Wiston, *Pray*, p. 79.

14. F.F. Bruce, *Commentary on Romans* (Grand Rapids: William B. Eerdman's, 1972), p. 79.

ticular candor of the total inability of even the most pious to pray. He used harsh words to attack the confident prayers that are considered divine, in which pious man strives to rise out of the depths and totally forgets how distant from the living God he is in his weakness and enmity."[15]

It was in the use of this particular gift that the Westminster Fellowship was able to acknowledge the fact that they did not know the depths of human need, and therefore all their intelligible prayers were sadly lacking. In this kind of super-rational intercession, the truth of Hans–Joachim Kraus's words gave expression to their experience: "In the dark life of this age, the heart lifted up by the Spirit cries out for the final revelation of the new creation for sonship and glory. These sighs are too deep for words because they cannot find any possibility of appropriate expression."[16] This is particularly true when intercession is made for others who are caught in the grip of disease and death. Many of the diseases that members of the Fellowship prayed for were judged incurable by medical science. How were they to pray in the will of God? The gift of tongues assisted them in this weakness. When bereavement was experienced, how were they to pray effectively without the ministry of this gift? There is so much about life that baffles us, leaving us sometimes in despair. It can be argued, of course, that one does not need to utter words of any sort, and the truth of this must be acknowledged. Nevertheless, man has a body as well as a spirit, and both aspects of his nature need to be involved in prayer. "The heart that God has probed contains nothing that could stand before Him, and could have any right and claim upon Him. Only through the Spirit are we now able to speak to God, but we are not speaking, He is speaking for us."[17]

*The Lord's Prayer.* Following the intercessory prayers, the Westminster Fellowship felt it appropriate to sum up their

---

15. Hans–Joachim Kraus, *The Threat and the Power* (Richmond: John Knox Press, 1966), p. 97.

16. Ibid.

17. Ibid., p. 103.

imperfect human prayers with the perfect prayer, which our Lord taught his disciples. When this was sung, rather than spoken, it had the effect of deepening faith, especially in the lines "For thine is the kingdom, the power and the glory forever, amen." The offering of this prayer often lifted the congregation to an exalted state of faith and expectation and the belief that the goodness of God would be expressed and his purposes fulfilled. Instead of this ancient prayer being a perfunctory exercise that many have grown to dislike because of over-familiarity, this beautiful, simple prayer of the Lord's became a medium through which the Fellowship expressed its confidence that God hears and answers prayer in his perfect will. Often as this prayer was sung, hands would be joined as a sign of the needed unity of the Spirit in prayer, along with the raising of the hands as a symbol of dependency upon him.

*Language.* The language of prayer is a matter of concern because Christian vocabulary needs to be free from that artificiality or literal correctness which has so often hindered the laity from feeling competent to pray aloud. Surely Stephen Winnard is right in his observation, "Do not ministers speak a highly exalted language which has helped to create the idea that the language used in addressing God is not the language of the average man?"[18] There is a real need to help evangelical Christians find freedom from those clichés which are so common to them. People need to be encouraged to be natural and personal in their prayers and to pray in the realization that God is with them, not in some faraway distant heaven. This is the spirit of the psalmist when he prayed and offered his intercession to God. Our Authorized Version, for example, has the psalmist say, "The heavens declare the glory of God and the firmament showeth forth his handiwork" (Ps. 24:1). But the Hebrew text is much more personal: "The heavens declare Thy glory God, and the firmament showeth forth Thy handiwork." This is the kind of personal prayer that is needed when praying to God. People need to improve their prayer language by not using the words "Father, O God, Jesus" as though they were

18. Stephen Winnard, *The Reformation of Our Worship* (Richmond: John Knox Press, 1964), p. 109.

punctuation marks between sentences. This may take some practice because many are so accustomed to this constant reference to the divine names. But if God is present, then we need to address him in as natural a way as a child to a father, not in some exalted, pedantic form of speech, which is unbecoming to one who knows the intimacy of God's love in Jesus Christ.

*Prayer and Symbolism.* Prayer also needs to make use of the symbolic aspects of the spiritual life. The Scripture shows us men at prayer taking many kinds of posture, i.e., kneeling, standing, prostrating, holding hands up high, covering the face, closing their eyes. All these are symbolic of the fact that God is holy and needs to be approached in a manner that speaks of complete reverence. Presbyterians need to recognize that they have been altogether too passive in their corporate prayers offered in church. People sit with their heads bowed and eyes closed, but no other symbolic act is required. In the new experience of God's presence in the Westminster Fellowship, discovery was made that the active use of the body helps to stimulate faith, giving a deeper manifestation of the inner reality of God. Kneeling can be very expressive of this, particularly the lifting up of hands. Paul enjoins Christians to "lift up holy hands to the Lord" (1 Tim. 2:8), and in this symbolic act of reaching up toward God they found themselves surrendering more easily to his will, adoring him with their hearts.

Other symbolic forms should be engaged in from time to time, depending upon the occasion. The great church festivals of the Christian calendar—Christmas, Easter, Ascension, Pentecost, Palm Sunday, Good Friday—are special calls to celebration, and the processional is one of the ways in which the whole congregation can be joined together in ministering to the Lord. As the Fellowship realized more and more that Jesus was with them in the power of his Spirit, worship services began to take seriously the fact that, although God is unseen, he is truly with his people. If it is true, as the Book of Revelation states so powerfully, that the saints and angels of heaven rejoice in God with a praise that is comparable to the noise of many waterfalls, then Christian worship on earth needs to be at least a reflection of that perfect heavenly worship. Rejoicing in God with all our hearts requires bodily expression of this inner reality. For the Westminster Fellowship, symbols became an important part of their worship, although they were conscious "that in the history of worship, twin dangers have occurred. Ceremonial is sometimes carried to excess and then in some situations there has been no ceremony at all. If it is exclusive and overelaborate, reformation will be stultified, but where it is lacking the deficiency must be supplied."[19]

Songs of praise and witness combined with prayers of confession, intercession, and thanksgiving indicate clearly that worship of God is primarily an act of prayer. Without the coming together of the church in prayer there can be no outpouring of the Spirit (Acts 2). Without the Spirit's action in the life of the Church's worship, Christ's people can do nothing.

---

## Chapter 4 (C)

Bruce, F.F. *Commentary on Romans.* Grand Rapids: William B. Eerdman's, 1972.

Butterick, Frank. *Prayer.* Nashville: Abingdon Press, 1942.

Castell, John. *Rediscovering Prayer.* New York: Association Press, 1955.

Hoon, Paul. *The Integrity of Worship.* Nashville: Abingdon Press, 1971.

Jasper, Ronald C.D., ed. *Renewal of Worship.* New York: Oxford University Press, 1965.

Kraus, Hans–Joachim. *The Threat and the Power.* Richmond: John Knox Press, 1966.

Laubach, Frank. *Prayer.* Westwood, New Jersey: Fleming and Revell, 1946.

Morrow, Thomas M. *Worship and Preaching.* London: Epworth Press, 1956.

Winnard, Stephen. *The Reformation of Our Worship.* Richmond: John Knox Press, 1964.

Wiston, Charles F. *Pray.* Grand Rapids: William B. Eerdman's, 1972.

---

19. Jasper, *The Renewal of Worship*, p. 52.

## (D) Involving the Laity in the Sacraments

One of the problematic areas in the life of a charismatic church is in the understanding and celebration of the Lord's Supper and Baptism. In the Presbyterian–Reformed tradition there has always been a strong emphasis upon the significance of the sacraments, although many in the Westminster Fellowship confessed that they joined the church without too clear an understanding of what it meant to have communion with Christ sacramentally. Thus they were challenged to rethink their tradition in the light of Scripture and Reformation discoveries, along with new expressions of truth, which are being restated by prominent theologians today. They discovered that there is much about the sacraments that is not conclusive. They were compelled by the very nature of the church to see that "the doctrine of the sacraments is today by no means a settled issue. Many questions are being raised that were supposedly answered long ago. The ferment that pervades practically the whole of dogmatics has also affected the doctrine of the sacraments."[1]

As the Fellowship began to examine the sacrament of the Lord's Supper, a growing sense of its importance began to take hold of them. Interest in remolding church traditions was not made for the sheer sake of change. The Westminster Fellowship identified very deeply with Bishop John Robinson, who expressed his own concern, "I confess to being increasingly conscious of the danger of liturgical revival for its own sake."[2] As a new congregation, they were particularly sensitive to the demands that some might make that they change so radically as to throw out the baby with the bath water.

All kinds of suggestions were made with respect to terminology as well as to practice. Some did not like the word *sacrament* and advocated *ordinance*. Others wanted the restoration of the time-honored word *eucharist*, but others shied

---

1. G.C. Berkouwer, *The Sacraments* (Grand Rapids: William B. Eerdman's, 1969), p. 13.
2. John A.T. Robinson, *Liturgy Coming to Life* (London: A.R. Mowbray and Co., 1960), p. 8.

away from it because it seemed too "Catholic." Vernard Eller, in his book *In Place of the Sacraments*, expressed the spirit of some people who felt that a whole new vocabulary was needed, perhaps a religionless approach entirely.[3] The congregation wanted to be true to the teaching and practice of Scripture, to the highest insights of Reformation theology, as well as to an understanding of the sacraments in terms of their present experience of the Holy Spirit. Anything they did in terms of sacramental observance had to affect the lives of the people in a realistic expression of their commitment to Christ. There was agreement with the Indian Christian scholar, Raimundo Pannikar, who, in emphasizing the need for reality in the worship of the modern Church, states, "Worship, if it is to really be what it claims to be and also to be of relevance, has to have a direct bearing on the life of the people."[4]

In the Presbyterian Reformed tradition there has been the observance of the Lord's Supper on a quarterly basis throughout the church year. At the beginning of the Westminster Fellowship's existence this practice was continued but gradually was changed to a monthly observance. Eventually they arrived at the position that the Lord's Supper should be observed every week, which was in keeping with the apostolic practice. It was discovered through the study of Reformation Church history and doctrine that Calvin had wanted to restore this sacrament to that of the original church but had been defeated in his desire by the elders at Geneva. Many of the writers on Reformed doctrinal practice in the modern Church agree with the statement by Oswald Millegan in his book on the ministry, that "unquestionably Calvin favored a weekly celebration and was only prevented from putting it into practice by the opposition of the civil powers."[5] All of this examination of the Bible and Reformation period encouraged the con-

3. Vernard Eller, *In Place of the Sacraments* (Grand Rapids: William B. Eerdman's, 1972), p. 16.

4. Raimundo Panikkar, *Worship and the Secular Man* (London: Orbis Books, Darton, Longman and Dodd, 1973), p. 56.

5. Oswald Millegan, *The Ministry of the Church* (New York, London: Oxford University Press, 1941), p. 98.

gregation to feel that they had to restore the Lord's Supper to this place of prominence, which it had at the beginning of the Christian movement.

As the Fellowship began to view the situation, there were several opinions held by the people as to the meaning of the sacrament. Some of Roman Catholic background were trying to break away from the traditional Roman view, but they nevertheless felt that Jesus was present in some way in the elements. Others of more Baptistic upbringing viewed it only as a memorial of Jesus' death, a time for giving thanks for what Christ had done for them at the cross. Those who had a Presbyterian heritage affirmed the Reformed tradition that Christ was real and present, but that this reality comes about only through the exercise of faith. What reaction was to be made to this variety of viewpoints, all held by members of a single congregation?

It was learned that the Reformed and other prominent leaders in the history of the Church never tried to explain what actually takes place in the Holy Communion but left it up to the individual believer to decide. Calvin had said, "The mode of this communion I refuse to discuss. It is too high a mystery either for my mind to comprehend or my words to express and to speak plainly, I rather *feel* than understand it."[6] Wesley also insisted that there was no value in speculating on its mystical meaning. He simply believed "that this divinity is so united to us . . ., but that union is utterly a mystery to me."[7] The Fellowship came to the conclusion that it is not necessary to have a perfect theological understanding as to the meaning of what happens in the Lord's Supper but rather that "if participation is engaged in devoutedly, regularly, and dutifully . . . it is much more important than a consideration of theoretical problems . . . of how the sacrament imparts to us the spiritual food of the body and blood of Christ."[8] The important thing for

6. David Cairns, *The Holy Communion* (London: SCM Press, 1947), p. 75.

7. Earnest Fiedler, *The Sacraments* (Nashville: Abingdon Press, 1969), p. 65.

8. Norman Pittenger, *Life as Eucharist* (Grand Rapids: William B. Eerdman's, 1973), p. 93.

the Westminster Fellowship was the realization that "we are fed by Christ and that He is surely present in the sacrament and thus in the experience of the devout communicant."[9] Indeed this study of the meaning of the sacrament made them realize "that the true reality of the sacrament is not the giving and eating of bread and wine, but the self-offering of Christ . . . with the external elements to attest this eternal reality."[10]

As study of the relevance of the Lord's Supper was made, the congregation identified with the Reformers, who "were so anxious to return to the primitive meaning of the Lord's Supper."[11] If they wanted to be true to the biblical pattern and to the highest concerns of some of the reforming fathers, it was important to be committed to the principle that the church must be "reformed and reforming." It was not some human inclination, this desire to restore the Lord's Supper to a weekly observance, but a spiritual impulse stimulated by the teaching of scripture.

The words of Karl Barth had come to our attention, in which we saw that the communion service is an integral part of worship. Yet there had been neglect not only by the Roman Catholic church but also by Reformed communions. He had stated,

> What we know today as the church service both in Roman Catholicism and in Protestantism is a *torso*. The Roman Catholic church has a sacramental service without preaching. We have a service with a sermon but without sacraments. Both types of service are impossible. . . . We do not any longer even realize that a service without sacraments is one which is outwardly incomplete. As a rule we hold such outwardly incomplete services as if it were perfectly natural to do so. What right have we to do that? We may ask the Roman Catholic church why she celebrates Mass without preaching, or without proper preaching, but we are asked ourselves what right we have to do what we do. Is there not a pressing danger that by omitting the

9. Ibid.

10. G.W. Bromiley, *The Sacramental Teaching and Practice of the Reformation Churches* (Grand Rapids: William B. Eerdman's, 1957), p. 83.

11. J.B. Philips, *Appointment with God* (New York: Macmillan Co., 1954), p. 9.

natural beginning and end of a true service the services we hold are incomplete inwardly and in essence as well . . . Why do the numerous movements and attempts to bring the liturgy of the Reformed church up to date—attempts and movements much spoken about all over the world today—prove without exception so unfruitful? Is it not just because they do not fix their attention on this fundamental defect, the incompleteness of our usual service, i.e., its lack of sacraments?[12]

In restoring the sacrament to this place of prominence the Fellowship hoped they could inspire other Reformed churches to follow suit. They realized that if renewal is to come to the whole Church, there needs to be a more serious attitude toward the scriptural pattern than is apparent in most Protestant churches. Most evangelicals boast of their Reformation heritage, "but the chief service for the Lord's Day has been entirely forgotten or disregarded."[13] At the same time they had no desire to follow the practice of some churches that are experiencing a liturgical renewal of the sacraments to such a degree that communion is observed so frequently it becomes "like a railway schedule . . . every hour on the hour, thus destroying any sense of parish solidarity and fellowship."[14]

The New Testament shows us a church of Christ's people who gathered regularly for the worship of the Risen Christ and who remembered his passion and death in this supper, which Christ instituted the night before his death. The writings of the early Church confirmed this, particularly the Didache, written before the end of the first century, which clearly instructed Christians to "gather yourselves together on the Lord's Day and break bread and give thanks."[15] There is a great need for Christians to realize that in the Lord's Supper we "approach the supreme service of the Church, her highest act of worship"[16] because,

12. Karl Barth, *The Knowledge of God and the Service of God* (London: Hodder and Stoughton Publishers, 1938), pp. 211, 212.

13. Pittenger, *Life as Eucharist*, p. 66.

14. Ibid., p. 65.

15. Donald Baillie, *The Theology of the Sacraments* (New York: Charles Scribners' Sons, 1957), p. 109.

16. Ibid.

properly understood, "the eucharist is the focus of Christian living."[17]

How should we observe this regular celebration of the Lord's Supper so that it will not become a repetitious ritual? Some Christians are a little wary about so frequent an observance because "this holy mystery never has seemed to mean what they had been led to expect, or what they felt it ought to mean. They continue to communicate out of a sense of duty or loyalty."[18] This fear need not continue if we are convinced that the meaningful celebration of Holy Communion will result in a deeper spiritual enrichment and strengthening of faith.

We should be grateful that the Reformation leaders did not lay down hard and fast rules for the observance of Holy Communion, although they all wrote liturgical orders of service, which were very similar and yet distinct from one another.[19] A variety of forms emerged, with their own particular style. This created a feeling of freedom to respond to the Lord as he led by his Spirit. The Westminster Fellowship studied a large number of Holy Communion services — everything from a contemporary Anglican form suggested by A.T. Robinson in his ministry to students at Cambridge to the contemplative forms prepared by V. Eller, who has theories about the replacement of the sacraments expressed from the viewpoint of the Brethren in Christ. The Fellowship felt free to let the Lord guide the congregation as it developed a Holy Communion service in a manner that was as meaningful to the congregation as possible.

As we have already stated, the singing of praise became a very integral part of the services of the fellowship. The offering of praise for a considerable period of time served to lift the hearts of the people emotionally and prepared them for the celebration of Holy Communion. Often they were so elevated in love and faith toward the Lord that it was the most natural thing to

---

17. Ibid.

18. Philips, *Appointment with God*, p. 5.

19. Bard Thompson, *Liturgies of the Western Church* (New York: New American Library, 1961), pp. 141–224.

move into the sacrament without any lengthy exposition of the Word, as had been their tradition.

This created a tension at first, because some felt this was too radical a break in their faithfulness to the Reformed practice. They knew that the Reformers had given a very prominent place to the preached Word before the receiving of Holy Communion. "Calvin asserts that for the right celebration of the Sacraments the Word is necessary . . . by this he means not only the reading, but the preaching of the Word, however brief this may be."[20] Dr. Geoffry Bromiley makes it clear in his book *On the Sacramental Teaching of the Reformation Churches* that the "Reformation Churches feel it necessary to maintain that the sacrament should not only be accompanied by the Word, but should be subordinate to it . . . there can be Word without Sacraments, but there cannot be Sacraments without the Word."[21] All Protestant writers of the Reformed tradition insist that the Word must be proclaimed before the sacrament is observed. "there cannot be a sacrament without it adhering to the evidence of the Word . . . the Word and the elements together make a Sacrament."[22] This was not an invention of the Reformation, for they recalled the older tradition of one of the great church fathers of the fourth century, Augustine, who said, "It is only when the Word is added that we have a sacrament . . . it is essential that the sacramental action should be in all practical circumstances accompanied by definite proclamation of the Gospel."[23]

In seeking to be true to this Reformed church heritage and yet not denying the reality of their discovery that faith is renewed through the singing of Scripture, the fellowship did not enter into the Holy Communion service without a brief message being proclaimed. A biblical word, such as *peace*, *reconciliation*, or *atonement*, might be taken and reflected on. With the reading

20. Cairns, *The Holy Communion*, p. 73.

21. Bromiley, *Sacramental Teaching and Practice*, p. 7.

22. Thomas Torrance, *The Mystery of the Lord's Supper* (Richmond: John Knox Press, 1958), p. 42.

23. Bromiley, *Sacramental Teaching and Practice*, p. 17.

of suitable Scriptures, which point to Christ in his death and Resurrection, they found the Holy Communion service to be a great opportunity for proclaiming the gospel and thus making it an evangelistic outreach. The readings were done by different lay people each week, and thus the sacrament was not centralized in the officiating pastor. There were an increasing number of people attending the services, some of whom had not yet responded in faith to Christ. The elders did not want them to come forward to receive Holy Communion without making a personal commitment of themselves to the Lord. The practice of "fencing the Table" was an old Reformation tradition with very somber overtones. But instead of frightening people by the serious words of invitation, "it was found that conviction of unworthiness is better produced by the sense of Christ's presence in our midst than by an attempt to catalogue the frailties of human nature."[24] Everyone is in need of the assurance of God's grace and forgiveness in Jesus Christ.

Along with this presentation of the Word in brief scriptural passages and exposition, lay people were also invited to share with the congregation how Christ had come into their lives and changed them. The giving forth of the Word in terms of personal experience witnessed to the reality of Christ and amplified the scriptural teaching that Christ has "procured for us the pardon and remission of sins . . . and is standing before us in His ever loving presence . . . willing to infuse us with His own glorified and still human life."[25] The Fellowship rejoiced that Sunday by Sunday people committed their lives to Christ as a result of hearing the gospel prior to the celebration of Holy Communion. There was a growing conviction that the sacrament was one of the most significant means through which the gospel could be preached and the unconverted called to faith in him. There was agreement with Oswald Millegan's insight, that "the sacrament is the most comprehensive expression of the whole gospel, the most complete revelation of God's initiative in the redemption of mankind, the most im-

---

24. Millegan, *The Ministry of the Church*, p. 108.
25. Ibid., p. 94.

pressive preaching of the cross as the means for human salvation that the church possesses. Here we have the most tender and heart-searching form of the Lord's invitation that we should come to Him, the penitent to find pardon, the sorrowing to find comfort, the weary to find rest."[26] Not only was there evangelistic outreach through the sacrament, but every believer was helped to sense the fact that all Christians are one in their common need of forgiveness, and this is the basis of the in-depth unity of the Church. "The basis for this community is the common Lordship of Jesus Christ, in whom all members have been granted forgiveness of sins."[27]

It is in the realization of the forgiveness of sins that there can be a true thanksgiving—a heartfelt eucharist. The spirit of thanksgiving flowed from the people because of this realization of God's grace. No longer could the Holy Communion service be a morbid remembrance of what Jesus had done nineteen hundred years ago. Many could remember how the sacrament of the Lord's Supper of past observances had seemed more like a funeral service, instead of a joyous time of praise overshadowed by the triumphant presence of Jesus. The infrequency with which Holy Communion had been celebrated "led to its solemn and awesome character . . . so that the spirit of worship which predominated the sacraments belonged to Good Friday rather than to Easter Sunday."[28] There had been so many conversions to Christ in the brief history of the Fellowship, particularly of people who had been out of the institutional church for many years, and this new awareness of joy and thanksgiving in the Holy Communion service was overpowering to them. Instead of sitting in solemn silence as before, the congregation would break forth into spontaneous praise, requesting songs that exalted the Lord Jesus in gratitude for all he was accomplishing in their lives. This was one of the high moments of praise, which was most fittingly expressed in song rather than in prose

---

26. Ibid.

27. Ernest B. Kroenker, *Worship in Word and Sacrament* (St. Louis: Concordia Publishing House, 1959), p. 32.

28. Cairns, *The Holy Communion*, pp. 68–69.

words. This kind of sacramental observance "called forth our response and gained the character it was originally designed to have—eucharistic thanksgiving, the greatest thanksgiving that the church offers in response to what God has done for us . . . we come with thanksgiving and in order to give thanks."[29]

This is not to suggest that the congregation had not been thankful before this, when they worshiped the Lord in a much more solemn manner. But what was happening now was more expressive of how they felt. They were joyful, therefore they displayed this in their outward attitude and in the songs that were sung. The Lord's Supper was not just a sacrament in which the death of Christ was remembered, but "it was the offering of life."[30] This spirit was not meant to rob the sacrament of the sense of mystery or ineffableness but, rather, to impart to it the "ineffability of the prodigal whose mouth was stopped by the father's kisses and the mystery of the father's heart which could be so big."[31] This is what eucharistic celebration is meant to be . . . a time of joyous thanksgiving in the knowledge of God's gracious forgiveness and full salvation. "It is not however, the kind of celebration encouraged by some modern liturgists who advocate a kind of superficial frivolity, instead of a celebration and festivity which is stimulated by the reality of the Gospel."[32]

Before the elements were given to the people, there was an act of consecration, in which both the symbols and the members of the congregation were dedicated to the Lord. This had no fixed form, which was in keeping with good Reformed church tradition, particularly that of the second century, where "the great eucharistic prayer appears to have had no obligatory fixed form."[33] This prayer has always been offered, as far as the Reformation church practice is concerned, by the ordained pastor. But as new appreciation for the priesthood of all believers deepened, it was seen that there is nothing inconsistent in involving the laity in the offering of this prayer. It

29. Millegan, The Ministry of the Church, p. 95.
30. Baillie, The Theology of the Sacraments, p. 117.
31. Eller, In Place of the Sacraments, p. 1.
32. Panikkar, Worship and the Secular Man, p. 59.
33. Evelyn Underhill, Worship (New York: Harper and Row, 1936), p. 240.

helped a few of the leading lay people to realize its importance and the significance of the permission which was being granted them. The Reformers had purged this prayer of all superstitious and erroneous elements[34] and had restored its original meaning. It was essentially a prayer calling upon the Holy Spirit "to act so that the Supper really becomes what Jesus Christ intended when He instituted it."[35] This prayer was then followed by a confession of the Apostles' Creed, which was a congregational act. The congregation was encouraged to realize that this confession "supplied the link of fellowship with our fellow believers of every race, tongue, as also with that great cloud of witnesses who trusted and were not confounded."[36]

When the elements were offered to the people, ample opportunity was again given to express the priesthood of every believer. Suitable words were spoken by the pastor or elders before the elements were given. And then, as the elements were passed from one to another, the people were also encouraged to speak to one another, "This is the Body of Christ broken for you. . . . This is the Blood of Christ shed for you," including other words of affirming faith. It is not only the pastor who can speak forth the "comfortable words of the Gospel," but believers can do this one to another.

As far as the elements were concerned, some inconsistency was practiced in the use of the bread and wine. Instead of using white bread, Jewish Passover unleavened bread was broken (matzos), which was felt to be more symbolic, linking the Lord's Supper with its roots in the Old Testament Passover meal. But as far as the "wine" was concerned, fermented grape juice was used instead. There were so many converted alcoholics in the congregation, it was felt appropriate to be sensitive to Paul's words in Romans 14:21 and not place a stumbling block before any weaker brother or sister. There was, however, the realization that "it is alien to the Reformed outlook to be

---

34. Bromiley, *Sacramental Teaching and Practice*, p. 52.

35. J.J. Von Allmen, *The Lord's Supper* (Richmond: John Knox Press, 1969), p. 30.

36. Millegan, *The Ministry of the Church*, p. 105.

scrupulously legal in matters of this kind."[37] The elements were passed from one to another, the bread being broken from a larger piece (to express the oneness of the Body) and the common cup to indicate the same truth. It was felt that "the custom of having bread cut into cubes has weakened the symbolism here."[38] When the priesthood of all believers is recognized, then both pastor and people have something to offer, and the words of Oswald Millegan become relevant: "When the service is carried out in accordance with what I believe to have been the original institution, they break the bread and give it to one another, and they drink of the common cup and give it to their neighbour."[39] In other words, everything that happens must enable each person to fulfill his own priestly ministry to the Lord and to the Body of Christ, as far as it is possible.

*The Peace.* The imparting of the ancient greeting, "The peace of the Lord be with you," should be given at this climactic moment in the Holy Communion Service, because there are always quarrels which need to be settled, and these are often between members of families or others present in the service. After receiving the reconciling love of Jesus, reaffirmed through the sacrament, it is much easier to seek reconciliation and forgiveness from those who have been hurt by us. When the Holy Communion service is observed in this manner, it enables broken relationships to be healed, which could otherwise continue to fester. One of the most unique methods to assist in this meaningful "wishing of peace" to one another is to move the chairs of the sanctuary to the side and then allow free movement so that members can go from one to another, breaking bread and wine together. This has proven to be one of the most spiritual moments in the lives of many who have needed to be restored to fellowship with a brother or sister. Charismatic renewal insists that love flow between members, and the Holy Communion service provides such an opportunity to take place. Peace becomes a reality, not just a word.

---

37. Bromiley, *Sacramental Teaching and Practice*, p. 71.
38. Millegan, *The Ministry of the Church*, p. 94.
39. Ibid., p. 96.

*Communion and Mission.* But the Lord's Supper is not just a time for fellowship between Christians and their Lord. We also participate in the worldwide fellowship of Christ's people on earth and in heaven. There is the responsibility to carry the love experienced at the Lord's table to the world. "Mission is not carried out for its own sake . . . one sows not for the sake of sowing, but in order to reap . . . it is from the Supper that the Church goes forth into the world."[40]

The Westminster Fellowship increasingly felt that they could not leave the sacred moment of Holy Communion without joining in prayer for the mission of Christ in the world. This took several forms in which people were invited to participate. Sometimes spontaneous prayer was offered from the congregation. On other occasions, "bidding prayers" were made. The leader would read forth particular areas of concern, such as "Let us pray for Christ's people suffering behind the Iron Curtain," or "Let us pray for those in ministry among prisoners." This was followed by silent prayer, in which members who exercised the gift of tongues were encouraged to pray quietly in this dimension. If someone wished to offer an audible prayer, they would do so, and then the leader would move from one request to another. All this served to involve the whole congregation in the concerns the Church had for the world and Christ's kingdom in this world.

*The Communion of Saints.* One of the aspects of Protestant church life that is sadly lacking is in our concept of the communion of saints. Although we confess that we believe in this reality stated in the Apostles' Creed, the average Protestant reacts to any thought of contemplating the memory of the "blessed dead." The Westminster Fellowship entered into this aspect of worship slowly, being reminded from Scripture that we "are surrounded by an innumerable company of witnesses" (Heb. 12:1). Everyone in the congregation had someone who had gone on to be with the Lord. How could they give recognition of their unity with them in the Body of Christ, temporal and heavenly? In the closing prayers of the Holy

---

40. Ibid., p. 100.

Communion service, they began to thank the Lord for the saints in heaven, making this into a very personal act of gratitude. Not only was thanks given for the Christians of the past, who have made their contribution to the life of the Church, but they began to be specific about their own loved ones. On the anniversary of the death of anyone in the Fellowship or anyone near and dear to someone, a special prayer of thanksgiving was offered. This was not just the bare reading of a name, but some information was given about the departed. This was not a matter of "glorying in men" but, rather, a praising of God for one of his faithful children who had blessed the lives of his family and the Church. This aspect of prayer was led by one of the laymen with other members taking part as they were inclined. The words of the Te Deum were sometimes used to sum up this communion of saints in prayer. Although this aspect of prayer is not widely practiced in Presbyterian churches, liturgists in the Reformed tradition are encouraging its restoration. "Prayers of thanksgiving should be offered for the departed, rejoicing in the communion of saints, we should give thanks for the great cloud of witnesses by which our earthly pilgrimage is surrounded and pray that we may likewise be followers."[41]

*Communion and the Second Coming.* The Sacrament of the Lord's Supper must be remembered as a sign or seal of Christ's presence, which will ultimately dissolve away in the fullness of the revelation of Jesus Christ in his Parousia. This is made clear when it is said, "We show forth the Lord's death, till He comes." This needs to be given greater prominence in the worship of the Church. It was felt in the Fellowship that they should close the communion by joining together in the ancient expression of Christian hope: "*Maranatha* (Even so come Lord Jesus)." This is not only a prayer expressive of our own personal yearning for his return but also an indication of the part we must all play in bringing about the final coming of his kingdom. A brief statement might be given about the nature of Christ's return, and then a number of things could take place. A brief

---

41. Ibid., p. 114.

paragraph from some outstanding Christian might be read; or a passage of Scripture that stresses the importance of his coming again; or a hymn that expresses this hope; or the singing of the Lord's Prayer, which conveys the longing that "thy Kingdom will come on earth as it is in heaven." All these liturgical forms can be utilized from time to time. The need to emphasize the coming again of the Lord in judgment and glory is significant for the church, because the Sacrament itself is only "a reminder that it is a profound and marvelous mystery . . . a ceremony belonging only to this world, to show forth the Lord's death till He comes."[42]

*The Sacrament of Baptism.* The sacrament of baptism is also one of the means of grace which is clearly observed in New Testament church life, and in the Reformed understanding of the church it occupies a special place. The Westminster Fellowship, as a charismatic church worshiping in the Reformed tradition, had many diverse attitudes toward the meaning of baptism. But a wonderful spirit of tolerance was practiced by the members. There was profound gratitude for this because, unfortunately, Protestantism has allowed the doctrine of baptism to be a most divisive factor, causing unnecessary separation between Christians. As a congregation that contained members from Roman Catholic, Reformed, and Baptist churches, the unity of the Body of Christ was emphasized, following the example of Paul in 1 Corinthians 1:13–17. It was therefore agreed that all three forms of baptism should be acknowledged as valid: sprinkling, pouring, and immersion. Those who wished baptism for their children were granted it, as well as the ceremony of dedication of children from families where infant baptism was not accepted.

In the administration of this sacrament, another opportunity to live out the priesthood of all believers was given. Prior to the formation of the Fellowship, the pastor had been responsible for the administering of this sacrament. Now it was felt that the whole church should participate. Anyone in the congregation who wished to join with the pastor in the laying on of hands

---

42. Philips, *Appointment with God,* p. 23.

was invited to come forward. Although the symbolic act of laying on of hands has been overlooked by most evangelical churches, there was agreement with J.K. Mozley, who writes, "The laying on of hands is the completion of baptismal ceremony . . . and has never been wholly obscured."[43]

It was a great joy to see grandparents, friends of the family, as well as members and officers of the church joining in prayer around the person being either baptized on profession of faith or presented by the parents. After the actual words of baptism were spoken, members were invited to offer prayer. Sometimes words of prophecy would come forth; which were cause for great joy on the part of parents or of the adult being baptized. Suitable verses of Scripture were often given as a special promise, and hymns were sung that had particular significance for the parents of the child or for the adult. This involvement of the whole church in this way delivered the baptismal service from mere ritual and gave additional testimony to the Body of Christ as a kingdom of kings and priests ministering together unto the Lord.

---

### Chapter 4 (D)

Allman, J.J. Von. *The Lord's Supper*. Richmond: John Knox Press, 1969.

Baillie, Donald. *The Theology of the Sacraments*. New York: Charles Scribners' Sons, 1957.

Berkouwer, G.C. *The Sacraments*. Grand Rapids: William B. Eerdman's, 1969.

Bromiley, G.W. *The Sacramental Teaching and Practice of the Reformation Churches*. Grand Rapids: William B. Eerdman's, 1957.

Cairns, David. *The Holy Communion*. London: SCM Press, 1947.

Eller, Vernard. *In Place of the Sacraments*. Grand Rapids: William B. Eerdman's, 1972.

---

43. J.K. Mozley, *The Gospel Sacraments* (London: Hidder & Stoughton, 1933), p. 76.

Fiedler, Earnest. *The Sacraments*. Nashville: Abingdon Press, 1969.

Kroenker, Ernest B. *Worship in Word and Sacrament*. St. Louis: Concordia Publishing House, 1959.

Millegan, Oswald. *The Ministry of the Church*. New York, London: Oxford University Press, 1941.

Mozley, J.K. *The Gospel Sacraments*. London: Hidder and Stoughton, 1933.

Panikkar, Raimundo. *Worship and the Secular Man*. London: Orbis Books, Darton, Longman and Dodd, 1973.

Philips, J.B. *Appointment with God*. New York: Macmillan Co., 1954.

Pittenger, Norman. *Life as Eucharist*. Grand Rapids: William B. Eerdman's, 1973.

Robinson, John A.T. *Liturgy Coming to Life*. London: A.R. Mowbray and Co., 1960.

Thompson, Bard. *Liturgies of the Western Church*. New York: New American Library, 1961.

Torrance, Thomas. *The Mystery of the Lord's Supper*. Richmond: John Knox Press, 1958.

Underhill, Evelyn. *Worship*. New York: Harper and Row, 1936.

---

## (E) Involving the Laity in the Exercise of the Gifts

Although there was a spiritual renewal within the Westminster Fellowship described as "charismatic," there was also the realization that a unique contribution to the life of the Church could be made that did not fit into a classical Pentecostal mold. There was a true appreciation for the Pentecostal church and its evangelistic outreach into the world, with its particular witness to the Spirit's availability. Nevertheless, the Westminster Fellowship knew, as a Reformed church, that they had a witness to make that could not be described in the theological language of the Pentecostal churches. They recognized that the historic roots of the Pentecostal church were linked with Wesleyanism and the Armenian understanding of the grace of God, whereas the Fellowship's understanding of the Christian life was associated with Calvinism and the classical sixteenth-century Reformation movement. What they wanted

117

at this particular point in their history was the unity of the Body of Christ in which each denomination could make its own contribution to Church renewal without being unfaithful to its own particular heritage or experience.

The pastor of the Westminster Fellowship had experienced the gift of tongues for many years prior to the so-called neo-Pentecostal movement. It had been an integral part of his prayer life but one that he had not shared widely with members of the church. What had taken place in his life seemed to be of such a sovereign action of God that he dared not require such an action on God's part to happen for everyone else. For many years he believed that the gifts of the Spirit were for only those whom God chose. He was sensitive to this kind of elitism, but it was still difficult for him to be associated with the charismatic renewal when it began to emerge in the historic churches in the 1960s. But, in spite of his own reluctance to share his experience, he was appreciative of what he saw happening in many areas of the Church's life across the world. Eventually he was compelled to "come out of the corner" and identify himself with the renewal of the Church charismatically, although it was with a certain amount of fear and concern for the unity of his congregation. He wanted to be faithful to Reformed theology, and yet he felt that there were some gaps in that theological approach which needed to be filled out.

Two books helped him at this time. One was by the Dutch theologian Hendrikus Berkhof, and the other was by Howard Erwin, a Baptist-trained minister at Princeton Seminary. These two books, *The Work of the Holy Spirit*, and *These Are Not Drunken As Ye Suppose*, respectively, made a plea for the restoration of the gifts of the Spirit to the life of the worshiping church. Erwin's book was a little more forthright than Berkhof's in its approach. Both the authors convinced the pastor that the Church could experience renewal in the manifestation of the spiritual gifts and still remain true to the Reformation understanding of the grace of God and the work of the Holy Spirit.

The outward expression of the gifts of the Spirit in all their fullness by the members of the congregation first took place in the small prayer meeting. There was general agreement with the insight of Stephen Winnard that "the best way to express the charismatic element in worship is to begin with the small-unit house church. This could also include the weekly prayer meeting or Bible Study."[1] This is where it began in the Fellowship, but they were not content for it to remain there and wanted it to become part of the worship experience of the gathered church on Sunday. The whole congregation was encouraged to take the Scripture seriously and to pattern church worship after an understanding of apostolic practice and not merely upon some traditional bias or cultural inclination.

They began to study the work of the Holy Spirit and to testify to his action in their lives. They began to realize that the Holy Spirit's ministry had been curtailed throughout the history of the church, "but it had never died out and reappears in every revival as a protest against the supposed formality and unreality of the liturgical routine, reasserting the freedom and direction of the action of the Spirit, the priesthood of the individual, and the prophetic office of preachers of the word."[2] What has taken place in the modern Pentecostal church and also in the neo-Pentecostal movement within the established churches is a sovereign renewal of these gifts by God himself. As the New Testament was studied, particularly the Acts of the Apostles and 1 Corinthians, the Fellowship felt that what they were discovering as a growing church was identical with the experience of the early Church. They rejoiced in this because for many of them the Acts of the Apostles had been merely a textbook on how God had acted in the primitive Church but was no longer today. Many of them had viewed the early Church nostalgically as the golden age of Christendom which would never return. With the organization of the structure of the church, the canonizing of Scripture, and the increased authority of the leadership, they had been taught that many of the extraordinary phenomena of the first century were no longer necessary. This was the position taken by the sixteenth-

---

1. Stephen Winnard, *The Reformation of Our Worship* (Richmond: John Knox Press, 1964), p. 82.
2. Evelyn Underhill, *Worship* (New York: Harper and Row, 1934), p. 88.

century Reformers, and this had been the Fellowship's understanding and indoctrination.

Then to their surprise they became aware of the reality of the gifts. They had not died out with the end of the apostolic age. "Charismatic worship is by no means set aside as the passing effect of unbalanced enthusiasm. On the contrary it was a genuine effect of Christian realism the importance of which is stressed in our earliest documents . . . witnessing to the presence and action of the quickening Spirit promised by Jesus to His Church."[3] The rationalism and dispensationalism of the Reformers could no longer be sustained on the basis of Scripture and Church history. Although the Fellowship did not have the scholarship of Michael Green to help them at the beginning, they were convinced that the curtailing of the Spirit's activity to the apostolic age was mere escapism, a refusal to expose the life of the Christian to the Spirit's powerful life. He remains sovereign in the Church and is not to be boxed up into any ecclesiastical compartment. "It is simply not the case that healing, prophecy, exorcism, and speaking in tongues, died out with the last of the apostles . . . there is plenty of evidence in the sub-apostolic days and periodically throughout the Church's history to show that these gifts did not die out . . . it is perfectly evident from the wide growth of the Pentecostal Church and the neo-Pentecostal movement in the last fifty years that God has poured out these gifts in rich measure on His people, rationalistic and skeptical though we have been about them."[4]

What did the Westminster Fellowship discover that helped them to become more open to the manifestation of the gifts of the Spirit in their worship and that kept them reformed in their understanding? They saw from their reading of Scripture that Jesus had given the Holy Spirit to his disciples on the day of his Resurrection (John 20:19–20) when he breathed on them and said, "Receive ye the Holy Ghost." In this action they were spiritually reborn. He then told them to wait for empowering by

---

3. Ibid., p. 234.
4. Michael Green, *I Believe in the Holy Spirit* (Grand Rapids: William B. Eerdman's, 1975), p. 198.

the Spirit in Jerusalem. This outpouring, or infilling, of the Spirit took place as the apostolic church gathered in the upper room for prayer (Acts 1; Acts 2:1–5). The experience of Pentecost was not the initial work of the Spirit but a continuation of his regenerating work. It was not a second work of grace but a sudden manifestation of his ministry, which released his power from within them. The Fellowship did not want to believe that there is something more to be added to the "fullness of Jesus," which he gives when he enters a person's life at the time of conversion. At the same time, the Reformed doctrine of sanctification does not rule out the growing awareness of the Spirit's presence in life, which can be described in terms of "something more." They had always thought of this progressive action as a movement forward into deeper consecration. But now they began to realize that a believer at a given moment – without being totally sanctified, as our holiness brethren teach – may be completely filled with the Spirit. This fullness will manifest itself in the release of spiritual gifts and the production of spiritual fruit.

They saw the Spirit's action in their lives as a kind of reactivation of faith or a release of Christ's reality, which manifested itself in a greater consciousness of his love and a much deeper love on their part for him. Instead of thinking of themselves as second-class Christians in comparison to those of the early Church, they saw themselves as one with them in everything that the Spirit imparted. With this conviction came the sense of expectancy that the gifts of the Spirit were available for all and could be released from them when they were willing.

The central problem for them at this time was how and where. They did not feel free to express the priesthood of all believers in this area of discovery within the regular service of worship on Sundays. Nor did they want to express these gifts in any manner that was inconsistent with their own temperaments. They had to depend on the Holy Spirit to show them the way and to help them enter fully into their new understanding of what he wanted to be in and through them.

One of the most helpful studies that engaged their attention was prepared by Father Donald Gelpi, *Pentecostalism – A Theological View*. Although it is written within the context of Catholic theology, they identified with much of his insight. The appendix contains a very orderly study of what it means to be involved in charismatic experience. There is nothing narrow or confining about his description of life in the Spirit. It helped to deliver them from the error of identifying the Spirit's release with the outward manifestation of speaking in tongues. A few of the congregation who had felt the new empowerment of the Spirit in their lives had not spoken in tongues for many months after their initial awakening. Although they grew in their appreciation of this gift, they did not make it the standard by which they judged whether a person was Spirit-filled or not. Indeed, they felt that Paul's words in 1 Corinthians 13 made it abundantly clear that love must be the test by which all the gifts are evaluated. Love must be seen as the primary manifestation of the Spirit's presence, without which the gifts are null and void. They were grateful for this insight and discovery because it saved them from the kind of pride that sometimes characterizes some in charismatic circles where the gifts are overemphasized. This attitude has created the undesirable quality of spiritual pride, thus erecting unnecessary barriers between those who function fully in the gifts and those who are limited in this area of spiritual ministry.

If the laity are to function with love in the gifts of the Spirit, they must be delivered from their prejudices. The charismatic movement, like every other movement in the history of the Church, has its negative as well as its positive side. If a congregation is going to be a channel through which the gifts can operate, they must be willing to "do all things decently and in order" (1 Cor. 14:41). This release of the Spirit in a worship service comes about not by manipulation or the utilization of carnal techniques but by a humble openness to the Word of God and the cooperation of the pastor.

When the Westminster Fellowship emerged, it provided the congregation with the opportunity and freedom to let the Spirit operate as he wills. As they continued in their study of the various books available on the work of the Spirit, in conjunction with the Bible itself, they saw that the gifts, if properly used, can strengthen the faith of God's people and give them a sense of expectancy toward him as they gathered for worship.

*Gifts of the Spirit.* In almost all their reading they had seen it

122

stated again and again that the gifts of the Spirit are allotted by God to certain individuals for a particular ministry. That is, some are given the gift of wisdom, some the gift of healing, some the gift of tongues, and so on. They began to realize that this attitude, rather than assisting a congregation to function boldly in the area of gift ministry, tends to inhibit them. As they studied 1 Corinthians 2, it seemed that the important word in the section was in verse 7, *manifestation*. The conviction began to jell around the awareness that every Christian has the Holy Spirit. "If you are a believer and have been baptized, then you are clothed with power from on High, but you may not have experienced or claimed the fullness of power."[5] The gifts are not the important thing to emphasize but, rather, the reality of the Spirit accompanied by a desire to be a channel through which he may operate. Instead of asking the Spirit to impart gifts, the members of the congregation were encouraged to rejoice in the indwelling presence of the Spirit, giving thanks for his presence and making themselves available to be used whenever he chose. It was this attitude more than any other that enabled them to eventually experience the manifestation of the Holy Spirit in their worship services.

As this approach was applied to the worship services, the people were encouraged to be sensitive to the promptings of the Spirit within them. As Stephen Winnard asserts, "because of the presence of the Holy Spirit in the life of the Church, grace has been given to each one according to the measure of Christ's gift. This means that the whole body of Christ is charismatic, equipped for the worship of God, as the Spirit quickens the heart and mind. This is why everyone should expect to contribute something to the life of the service and not to remain silent and passive."[6]

This is the key. As the pastor stressed the importance of each member, acknowledging his priesthood as a believer and showing his willingness to step aside as a dominant figure in the

---

5. Elmo Agrimson, *The Gifts of the Spirit and the Body of Christ* (Minneapolis: Augsburg Press, 1974), p. 106.

6. Winnard, *The Reformation of Our Worship*, p. 116.

service, the gifts began to manifest themselves. The most difficult problem to overcome was the cultural reticence and inhibition of the members. But as they felt more at home in the atmosphere of love, which prevailed in the services, natural fears began to diminish, and gift manifestation began to take place.

They found that the gifts of tongues, prophecy, and interpretation would manifest themselves after a time of singing followed by silence, or after the preaching of the Word of God followed by silent meditation, or during times of special ministry to people—e.g., baptism, recommitment of faith, prayers for healing. The gifts of the Spirit emerged according to the needs of the people. If a person confided in the congregation a need for prayer in making a decision, the gift of wisdom would be manifested. If a person wanted discernment, then the gift of knowledge and discernment would be expressed. Sometimes people were so obviously upset by a problem that it was necessary to exercise the gift of exorcism. God called forth his gifts in order to strengthen.

The significant thing to note is that where there was a spirit of expectancy, the gifts were manifested very readily. The idea that only a certain person has a particular gift and will manifest it all the time is not necessarily true or to be expected. It is healthier when the Spirit is expected to call forth the gifts as he chooses. It helps to deliver people from the prideful spirit, especially if they function in one of the more spectacular gifts. It was discovered that a person might manifest the gift of tongues one Sunday and not operate in that gift for many months. A prophecy might be given by someone who would not speak again for a considerable period of time. A person who may have been unresponsive on one occasion would be surprised to find himself being a faith builder on another occasion. In other words, they found it much more biblical not to emphasize that every person has a certain gift but, rather, to encourage people to earnestly desire gifts (1 Cor. 14:1) and then to permit themselves to be open to the leading of the Spirit at all times. With this attitude at work, many in the congregation manifested all the gifts from time to time, depending on the occasion, whether it was at church worship or during the week in some particular situation. This helped a great deal to keep a person from imagining that the Spirit wanted to function through them in only one or perhaps two gifts but nothing else. The Spirit is sovereign and can work through whom he chooses and on any occasion.

If a congregation is encouraged to cultivate the spirit of expectancy, it is truly surprising what takes place in a service. What is needed above all things is an atmosphere of acceptance, which sets people at ease and makes them willing to be channels of the Spirit's activity. Evelyn Underhill forcefully reminds us in her book *Worship* that "whenever the institutional life stiffens and becomes standardized there is a reaction toward that primitive group enthusiasm and prophetic ministry which is described in the New Testament."[7] What is needed is to keep the gifts of the Spirit in harmony with all the other aspects of worship and not to overemphasize their importance, as the Corinthian church did until corrected by the apostle Paul. Again, Evelyn Underhill underscores the conviction: "We do not get a balanced view of worship in the apostolic church unless we remember that it practiced together and held in equal honor the sacramental and pneumatic, liturgic and prophetic responses to God in Christ."[8] "Again, these two aspects are not to be sharply divided but are best understood as completely opposites of one experienced reality and it is still true that the fullest and deepest worship uses both. In both, God is acting in and on His Church . . . and together they witness to the central fact that He is tabernacled among men and justifies the mingled exaltation and intimacy of Christian response."[9] It was the latter part of this statement which was such a source of joy for the Westminster Fellowship. It was in the exercise of the gifts of the Spirit that they became deeply aware of the promised presence of Jesus with his people. It was in the experience of this reality that worship flowed toward God with deep gratitude, with a sense of awesome wonder that he has actually manifested

7. Underhill, *Worship*, p. 89.
8. Ibid., p. 234.
9. Ibid.

himself to his people today, as he did to the apostles of old. It had the effect of closing the gap between the first century and the twentieth, making them feel a truly apostolic people.

If the gifts of the Spirit are to be an accepted part of congregational worship, "then the minister who is concerned to improve the liturgy of his congregation should begin to meet regularly with those in his congregation who show any sign of being willing to be involved in the services. There is no one part of the service where trained laymen could not be employed. They may differ from week to week so that no one person is given the feeling that he or she is called to preach, teach, lead singing, etc."[10] This would also include the exercise of the gifts. Training is necessary if people are to function in this ministry effectively. This is not a mechanical departure from spontaneity but simply enables people to understand how they may be as helpful as possible to the whole Church. Above all, there must be a willingness to be used, and then God will call forth his gifts as he pleases for the upbuilding of his people.

---

## Chapter 4 (E)

Agrimson, J. Elmo. *Gifts of the Spirit and the Body of Christ*. Minneapolis: Augsburg Press, 1974.

Berkhof, Hendrikus. *The Work of the Holy Spirit*. Richmond: John Knox Press, 1964.

Erwin, Howard. *These Are Not Drunken As Ye Suppose*. Plainfield, New Jersey: Logos, 1968.

Ford, J. Massingberd. *The Pentecostal Experience*. New York: Paulist Press, 1970.

Gelpi, Donald L. *Pentecostalism—A Theological Viewpoint*. New York: Paulist Press, 1971.

---

10. Winnard, *The Reformation of Our Worship*, p. 153.

Green, Michael. *I Believe in the Holy Spirit*. Grand Rapids: William B. Eerdman's, 1975.

Jones, James, and William, M. *Filled with New Wine*. New York: Harper and Row, 1974.

Olson, William George. *The Charismatic Church*. Minneapolis: Bethany Fellowship, 1974.

Williams, Rodman. *The Pentecostal Reality*. Plainfield, New Jersey: Logos, 1972.

# An Order of Service Used by the Congregation of the Westminster Fellowship, in New Westminster, British Columbia

The people being assembled, and in an attitude of prayer and meditation fitting for the commencement of divine worship, the pastor assumes his place on the chancel and greets the people.

M. The Lord be with you.

C. And with you also.

(or some suitable Christian greeting)

The worship of God is explained. Why we have come together:

To worship God the Creator

To rejoice in the revelation of himself in Jesus Christ

To open our hearts to the Holy Spirit

Suitable verses of Scripture are given, such as:

John 14:6

John 4:24

Psalm 98:1

This is followed by *silence* as the congregation *meditates* on the reality of the Lord or brief sentences of Scripture or while portions from Christian writers are read, emphasizing his presence. Silence should not be hurried, and there should be intervals of at least forty-five seconds to a minute between the spoken statements.

God is in his holy temple, let all the
earth keep silence before him.
Be still and know that I am God, I will
be exalted above the heathen;
I will be exalted on the earth, come
ye apart and rest awhile.

*Sursum Corda*

M. Lift up your hearts.
C. We lift them up to thee.

*Prayers of Thanksgiving*: The pastor encourages each person to speak forth a word of praise and thanksgiving for any and every blessing in life. These words should be brief, followed by the singing of "Praise God from Whom All Blessings Flow."

*Praise in Song*: We are then reminded how God wants his people to praise him. Led by our choirmaster, we have a prolonged period of praise (thirty to forty minutes) which includes psalms — old and newly written ones; hymns — ancient, traditional, as well as contemporary; spiritual songs — spontaneous songs sung in the Spirit (Eph. 5:18). Hymns are followed by silence; hymns may be requested by the people. As much as possible, we encourage people to sing without the use of their books. This enables people to respond to the Lord with the raising of hands and the clapping of hands, as the Spirit leads each worshiper.

The hymns set forth the mighty acts of God:
  The creation of God
  The birth of Jesus
  The person of Jesus
  The Crucifixion and Resurrection
  The Second Coming of Jesus
  The Holy Spirit and the kingdom
In other words, the hymns are objective expressions of praise, not hymns of witness.

The praise very naturally leads to the most exalted moment in the service, which is the Communion of the Lord's Supper:
  The Gospel story of Christ's death is read

130

A brief message explaining the meaning of his death and the Lord's Supper

Invitation to approach him in complete faith and trust

Prayers of consecration – the Apostles' Creed

People invited to come forward

Pastor and elders give them the elements accompanied by suitable verses of Scripture

Those sitting in their seats are led by the organist and choirmaster in the singing of suitable hymns

Following the Holy Communion, the people stand and offer to the Lord the spontaneous praise and prayer of their hearts, either silently or verbally, as the Spirit indicates.

This is usually an occasion for such response to the Lord that the gifts of the Spirit manifest themselves in prophetic utterance, tongues and interpretation, and thanksgiving.

The Peace
Given to one another, with the embrace of Christian love.

Then follows a time of informal fellowship, in which the congregation meet one another around the coffee table – a most significant time in which people are welcomed in a very personal way.

Service resumes with silence

Invocation

Psalms and hymns are sung

Responsive readings or litanies, using
Book of Psalms (RSV)
*Good Lord, Where Are You?* – Contemporary psalms
Ancient hymns are sung – The Magnificat, Te Deum

Scripture is read – sometimes by all the people in unison or by a person other than the pastor.

Prayer of illumination – sung or spoken

The Sermon

Dedication of ourselves to the Word of God

Expression of faith, in the Apostles' Creed
  Prayers of commitment — bidding prayers, silent prayer

The Offering — praise is sung during the receiving of it.
  Hymns of praise or special music

Body Life Ministry — a time of sharing, responding to what God has said in the service, or — during the week — prayers for the sick and the laying on of hands
  Intercession for special needs
  Prayer for the world, the Church, one another (These prayers are offered by the spiritual leaders of the church.)

The Lord's Prayer — sung

Benediction

Suitable Sung Doxologies